PHILOSOPHY AND MIRACLE
The Contemporary Debate

PHILOSOPHY AND MIRACLE
The Contemporary Debate

David Basinger
and
Randall Basinger

Problems in Contemporary Philosophy
Volume 2

The Edwin Mellen Press
Lewiston/Queenston

Philosophy and Miracle: The Contemporary Debate by David and Randall Basinger

This is volume 2 in the continuing series
Problems in Contemporary Philosophy
Volume 2 ISBN 0-88946-327-1
PCP Series ISBN 0-88946-325-5

 For information contact:

The Edwin Mellen Press
Box 450
Lewiston, New York
USA 14092

The Edwin Mellen Press
Box 67
Queenston, Ontario
L0S 1L0 CANADA

Printed in the United States of America

ACKNOWLEDGEMENTS

Acknowledgement is made to the following journals in which some of this material appeared in a different form:

"Miracles as Violations: Some Clarifications," *The Southern Journal of Philosophy* 22 (1984): 1-7. Used by permission.

"Flew, Miracles and History," *Sophia* 22 (July, 1983): 15-22. Used by permission.

"Christian Theism and the Concept of Miracle," *The Southern Journal of Philosophy* 18 (1980): 137-50. Used by permission.

"Miracles and Apologetics: A Response," *Christian Scholar's Review* 9 (1980): 348-53. Used by permission.

"Science and the Concept of Miracle," *Journal of the American Scientific Affiliation* 30 (December, 1978): 164-68. Used by permission.

TABLE OF CONTENTS

PREFACE

Miracles have always played an important role in the thoughts and lives of classical Christian theists. It should not be surprising, therefore, that philosophers of religion have always found the concept of miracle to be of interest. In recent years this has especially been true of those philosophers of religion within the analytic tradition. This book represents our assessment of these recent discussions.

In one sense what is found in this volume is truly a collaborative effort. The material reflects a fifteen year dialogue (which produced along the way two doctoral dissertations and a master's thesis related to the miraculous). And we are both in agreement with all that is written. But we are not equally responsible for the form in which all the material appears. David is primarily responsible for the content and structure found in Chapters I and IV. Randall is primarily responsible for the content and structure found in Chapter V. And we together generated what is found in Chapters II and III.

Finally, we would like to thank Marie Mercer for patiently typing draft after draft while this manuscript was in preparation.

David Basinger
Rochester, New York

Randall Basinger
Grantham, Pennsylvania

CHAPTER I

What is a Miracle?

I

WHAT IS A MIRACLE?

The term 'miracle' is used in normal discourse to refer to a wide variety of states of affairs. Some individuals, for example, use the term to describe any unexpected occurrence—from the completely unexpected passing of an exam to the rediscovery of a hopelessly lost article to the rapid, welcomed change in a person's behavior.

Others use the term in a more restricted sense. They allow only those very unusual events which apparently conflict with known scientific laws—events such as the recent survival of a 10,000 foot fall by a stewardess or the rapid, complete recovery of a person dying of cancer—to be labeled miraculous.

But 'miracle' is most frequently defined in a religious sense. That is, for most individuals, to say that an event is a miracle is to say not only that it was in some sense unusual but also that it was the result of some sort of divine activity. Moreover, it is this religious sense of the term which has generated the greatest amount of philosophical discussion. And, thus, it is this sense of the term with which we will be concerned.

In this chapter, our purpose is twofold. We shall clarify what it has meant for most philosophers and theologians to claim that a miracle is 'an unusual event caused by a god' and also analyze the various philosophical problems which such definitional interpretations have generated.

Miracles as acts of god

The term 'god' has a wide variety of meanings. For some it is simply a synonym for the spirit of love in the world. For others god is 'everything', or he (it) is 'nothingness'. Within the context of miracle, however, we can be more specific. A miracle is normally considered an event which has been brought about for a specific purpose—for example, to help someone in need, demonstrate a divine presence, etc. Miracles are also normally considered events which could not be performed solely by humans (although it is often allowed that miracles can be performed by gods *through* humans). Furthermore, although many individuals believe that superhuman acts can be performed by malevolent agents, and some believe that gods appear in visible forms, the term 'god' is usually reserved for those benevolent, invisible agents who function as the recipients of religious worship.

Accordingly, to say that a miracle is an event caused by god is normally to say, at the very least, that it is an event caused by a benevolent, invisible, rational agent who is more powerful than humans and is worshiped by them. It should be noted, however, that when most analytic philosophers discuss miracles, they have an even narrower concept of god in mind. They are normally concerned with the classical Christian God: a being who in addition to being an invisible, rational object of worship is also considered the omnipotent, omniscient, perfectly good creator of all. And, thus, this is the concept of deity on which we will concentrate our efforts.

But what exactly does it mean to say that such a being has caused a given state of affairs? Most classical Christian theists believe that all states of affairs are acts of God in the sense that God has created the universe, established the 'laws' upon which causal interaction within this universe is based and continues to sustain such interaction by his power. In this sense, the birth of a baby or a fire in a forest or a given rainstorm can all be said to be acts of God. But most classical Christian theists also maintain that there are some events—for example, answers to prayer, healings—which would not have occurred in the exact manner in which they did if God had not *directly* intervened—that is, if God had not at some point in some manner directly circumvented or modified the general cause/effect patterns he has established. Miraculous states of affairs, not surprisingly, are normally considered to fall within this 'direct act of God' category.

This concept of direct divine causation, though, has not gone unchallenged. All adequate (or complete) causal explanations, some philosophers argue, must be scientific in the sense that they stipulate a set of necessary and sufficient empirical conditions for the occurrence of the events in question. But since divine influence is, by definition, nonempirical, any state of affairs which has been identified as a direct act of God has at least one necessary causal factor that is nonempirical. Accordingly, the argument concludes, no 'supernatural' explanation can be truly scientific and, thus, adequate.[1]

One aspect of this argument seems acceptable. The antecedent causal conditions related to alleged direct acts of God—e.g., prayers, etc.—are often observable as are the alleged results—e.g., a healed body. But God is, by definition, incapable of detection by the human senses or their extentions. Thus, if an adequate causal explanation can stipulate only empirical causal factors, then direct acts of God can be given no adequate explanation.

But why ought we acknowledge that all adequate (or complete) *causal* explanation must be scientific? Such a contention seems for some to be based on the assumption that all observable occurrences have, in principle, solely empirical antecedent causal conditions. But such an assumption is unwarranted. It has not been demonstrated conclusively to the satisfaction of the majority of rational individuals that there is no God or that God, if he exists, *could* not intervene in earthly affairs. Thus, divine causation remains a logical possibility. And if divine causation is a logical possibility, then it is possible that some events contain nonempirical causal factors. And this being the case, it cannot be argued that all causal explanations must be scientific. Or, to state the point more succinctly, given that we cannot categorically rule out the possibility of nonempirical causal conditions for some observable phenomena, we cannot justifiably maintain that all causal explanations must be stated only in terms of necessary and sufficient empirical causal conditions.

But perhaps to respond in this manner is to miss the essential point. Someone might readily acknowlege that divine causation is possible but argue that we simply cannot gather enough information about such causation to obtain anything close to an adequate understanding of it. That is, someone might argue that since supernatural causal explanations cannot be verified through empirical testing, they have less predictive accuracy than scientific explanations and, thus, are not as adequate functionally.

This claim may well be correct. It may well be that scientific and supernatural explanations cannot be considered on a functional par with respect to their ability to 'explain' and 'predict' event types. And we certainly ought not allow supernatural explanation to be substituted at will for its scientific counterpart.

But the fact remains that supernatural causation is possible. And if supernatural intervention does occur, only a nonscientific 'supernatural' form of explanation can incorporate the necessary nonempirical causal factors involved.

Miracles as 'unusual events'

Exactly how unusual or extraordinary must a direct act of God be before it can be labeled miraculous? Since the time of Hume, it has been most popular in philosophical circles to define miracles as direct acts of God which 'violate' natural laws. But what exactly does it mean to say that a natural law has been violated? As we shall see, this is actually a very complex, debatable issue. However, it is possible to state what most philosophers and theologians seem to have in mind.

Natural laws, at least since the time of Hume, have basically been understood to be descriptive generalizations which tell us what will or will not happen (or what almost certainly will or will not happen) under certain conditions.[2] Well-established generalizations of this sort are thought to tell us, for example, that water does not turn instantly into wine and that those who have truly died do not (at least in a physical sense) come back to life. But let us assume that someone actually were to turn water instantly into wine or rise from the dead. We would then be forced to acknowledge the occurrence of an event which well-established natural laws clearly tell us will not occur. And to be forced to acknowledge the occurrence of such a counterinstance is what most philosophers and theologians seem to have in mind when they talk about what it would mean to be 'forced' to acknowledge that a natural law has been violated.

Some philosphers, however, believe that to conceive of a violation of a natural law in these terms is incoherent. Alistair McKinnon, for example, maintains that since natural laws are simply "shorthand descriptions of how things do, in fact happen"—i.e., shorthand descriptions of the actual course of events"—to claim that an occurrence is a violation of a natural law is to claim that the event in question is a "suspension of the actual course of events." And such a state of affairs, he points out, is of course an impossibility. Events may well occur, he acknowledges, which seem at present to be incompatible with how we believe things normally happen. But a true counterinstance to what we now believe to be a natural law only shows the law to be inadequate. Since natural laws, by definition, describe "the actual course of events," we must in principle always be willing to expand our laws to accommodate any occurrence, no matter how unusual. We can, by definition, never have both the exception and the rule.[3]

Antony Flew offers us a similar line of reasoning. To say that an event is a violation of a natural law is to say that it is a true counterinstance to a true nomological. But a true nomological, he informs us, is a logically contingent universal proposition, that is, a proposition which states that "certain things in fact must happen or in fact cannot happen." Accordingly, he argues, a true nomological can have no true counterinstance. If a true counterinstance (C) to a *current* nomological (N) has in fact occurred, N no longer accurately tells us what in fact cannot happen and, thus, can no longer be considered a true nomological. And C, accordingly, cannot be considered a true violation. On the other hand, if it is maintained that N is a *true* nomological—that is, does accurately tell us what cannot happen—then C cannot be considered a true violation. In short, Flew, like McKinnon, argues that once we properly understand the inviolable universality of natural laws, we will see that we can acknowledge no 'exceptions' to such 'rules'.[4]

Such reasoning is in one sense quite problematic. It is true, as Flew and McKinnon suggest, that scientists must assume as a working hypothesis that current nomologicals express what will always happen under certain conditions. And they are also correct in arguing that any apparent counterinstance to a current nomological necessitates a reevaluation of the 'law' in question. But as many philosophers have recently pointed out, natural laws are not merely summary statements of what does in fact happen. Nor do they describe in some *a priori* fashion what in fact can or cannot happen. Natural laws, rather, only describe events in so far as they take place in a *predictable and regular manner*.[5]

Thus, there is no need to agree with Flew and McKinnon that when faced with a seeming counterinstance, we are under some mandate to either admit that the event occurred as reported and abandon the relevant nomological or affirm the relevant nomological and deny that the event actually occurred. If a seeming counterinstance proves to be repeatable, then the current laws in question certainly must be abandoned (or modified). But, otherwise, we can, in principle, affirm both the counterinstance and the law.

For example, let us assume that a cup of water turns instantly into wine. If this state of affairs were shown to be repeatable—that is, if we could demonstrate that under certain conditions water would always turn instantly into wine—then our current nomologicals describing the properties of water (which do not allow us to predict this phenomenon) would of course have to be abandoned. But if there were in fact good objective evidence that the phenomenon had occurred and it could *not* be shown to be repeatable, there is no reason why we should feel compelled to either deny that the water had actually turned into wine or abandon our current nomologicals which describe the properties of water. It would be more reasonable in this case for the scientist to continue to assume for practical purposes that the relevant laws were valid and simply view the seeming counterinstance in question as an anomalous, presently unexplainable event. To do so would not, as Flew implies elsewhere, render the nomologicals in question nonfunctional or turn science into a quasi-metaphysical guessing game. For as long as this recalcitrant event was not repeatable, it would furnish us with no basis upon which to build an alternative to the current laws in question. Such laws could (indeed, would need to) remain the working hypotheses which the scientist utilizes.

But can we justifiably maintain that such nonrepeatable counterinstances (exceptions) are *true violations* of the relevant natural laws? The answer to this question, we shall see, depends upon the type of causation presupposed. Let us assume that an event (E) is incompatible with a well-established set of laws (L). And let us further assume that E had some cause, that is, let us assume E was not an uncaused event. It appears we are left with three possible causal explanations for E.

First, it is possible that some undetected (possibly unknown) natural causal force or factor was present and that this force or factor, either apart from or in conjunction with the natural conditions presupposed in L, caused E. For example, let us assume again that a glass of water turns instantly into wine. One possibility is that some undetected (and possibly undetectable) natural causal force or factor combined with the known properties of water to create the wine.

If this were the case, would there be any basis for claiming that L—that 'law' which states that water does not turn into wine—has been violated? We believe not. Natural laws—even those which are considered universal—are conditional propositions. They do not describe what will or will not occur, given *any set* of preconditions. Natural laws tell us that, given a specific set of natural conditions *and given that there are no other relevant forces present*, certain natural phenomena will or will not always occur.

For example, there are no natural laws which tell us, strictly speaking, that water will not immediately turn into wine under *any set* of possible conditions. Such laws tell us only that given a certain set of specified natural conditions—e.g., given water with normal properties and normal atmospheric conditions—water will not turn into wine.

Accordingly, if a seeming counterinstance (E) to a well-established set of laws (L) were the result of some undetected natural force—for example, if water were turned into wine by some natural force which science has yet to identify—it would in no meaningful sense follow that L has been violated. For that set of natural conditions under which E occurred would not in this case be identical with that set of identifiable natural conditions under which it is maintained in L that E-type events will not occur. What would follow rather is only that the explanatory and predictive powers of L were in this context inadequate (not exhaustive). In short, if E were the result of some natural causal factor which science has yet to identify, E and L would remain, in principle, perfectly compatible.

But what if E is at least in part the result of some supernatural causal force? What if, for example, water is turned immediately into wine by some god who desires to demonstrate his power. Can we then say that those well-established natural laws which declare that this will not occur have been violated? A growing number of philosophers believe so. In fact, Douglas Odegard has recently argued that we can *only* "justifiably claim that an event is a violation (if) we have good reason to believe that it is produced by a god."[6] But on the basis of what has already been stated, we can see that such reasoning is misguided. It is certainly true that if we could establish that an event (E) had been caused (at least in part) by a supernatural force, then no totally natural explanation for E as an *event token* could be forthcoming. But since natural laws only state what will or will not occur under certain natural conditions, they cannot be used to predict or explain what will happen when nonnatural forces are present. Thus, while it would certainly be correct to maintain in this context that our current set of natural laws describing the activities of water would be shown to be inadequate (non-exhaustive) if water were turned into wine by a god, it could not be said that this event was a violation of such laws. The 'counterinstance' and the natural laws in question would again be perfectly compatible.

But what if E occurred even though there were no undetected natural or supernatural causal factors present. That is, what if E occurred given only the natural conditions presupossed by the relevant laws? For example, let us assume that water has turned immediately into wine, given the exact natural conditions under which our relevant natural laws tell us this will not occur. Could we then meaningfully claim that the relevant natural laws have been violated? It might appear that we still could not. Since in the present context we are assuming that E has occurred given the exact natural conditions under which the relevant set of laws (L) states that events like E will not occur, it might appear that L must be abandoned or modified and, thus, that E could not be considered a violation. But the situation is more complex. If it is true that water has turned into wine under the exact conditions our current laws state it will not, then such laws are, of course, weakened. For example, they can no longer be considered universal propositions. And it is, of course, true that if this phenomenon can be shown to be repeatable naturally, the relevant laws must be abandoned or modified.

But let us assume that although water does once turn into wine under the natural conditions assumed in L, this occurrence is not repeatable. And let us further assume that L is a set of very well-established laws and that no other set of laws can be found which can accommodate this phenomenon and is equally simple and useful. In this case, it seems to us, it would be justifiable to continue for *practical purposes* to consider L a valid set of natural laws. And, thus, in this case it would make sense to claim that L has been violated, for in this and only this case would we actually be saying that the rule and the exception exist simultaneously. Or stated differently, in this and only this case would be saying both that E-type events do and do not occur under the same set of natural conditions.

We must conclude then that philosophers such as Richard Swinburne who argue that miracles (defined as acts of God) can, in principle, justifiably be labeled violations are incorrect.[7] It is correct to argue—against Flew and McKinnon—that if an event (E) appears to be a nonrepeatable counterinstance to a well-established set of laws (L), we are not compelled to choose between abandoning L or contending that E has not occurred as reported. And it may be that some nonrepeatable counterinstances could justifiably be labeled acts of God.

But a nonrepeatable counterinstance caused by God would not, if it were to occur, be a *violation* of the nature laws in question. For, as we have seen, it is only if a nonrepeatable counterinstance were to occur under the exact set of *natural* conditions presupposed by such laws that it could in any meaningful sense be considered a violation. And events directly caused by God do not, by definition, occur under just that exact set of *natural* conditions presupposed in any set of natural laws.

But this fact may be of little theological importance. When theists maintain that miracles are violations of natural laws, most of them mean simply that miraculous events will never have natural explanations available for them. But to hold that a direct act of God is *permanently inexplicable* in this sense does not commit one to the incoherence involved in maintaining that a direct act of God is a *violation* of a natural law in the sense in which we have been defining the term. Direct acts of God cannot be violations because an event can only be a violation of a natural law, strictly speaking, if there are no nonnatural causal factors involved. But to say that an event is permanently inexplicable in the sense in question is only to say that the scientific enterprise will never formulate a natural covering law under which events of this type can be subsumed. And to affirm that an event falls into this category is consistent with maintaining that it was caused by God.

Or,to state this important point somewhat differently, events of a certain type might be permanently inexplicable scientifically for at least three reasons: because they are direct acts of God, because science will never be able to identify all the natural causal factors or because what normally happens under a given set of natural conditions simply did not happen. But an event can be said to violate a law for only one of these reasons: because what 'always' happens under a given set of natural conditions did not happen under this exact set of natural conditions. Thus, the fact that we cannot consistently predicate supernatural causation of an event which is considered a 'violation' in no way entails that we cannot coherently claim that other types of events have supernatural causal components and for that reason could never be completely explained scientifically.[8]

Moreover, it is primarily the alleged fact that an occurrence can be given no natural explanation (is permanently inexplicable), not the alleged fact that the relevant natural laws are intrinsically inadequate (have been violated), which lends credence to the theistic claim that the event in question was caused by a god. So the theist loses no potential apologetical value by defining the miraculous as a permanently inexplicable event rather than as a violation.

Accordingly, it appears that those theologians and philosophers who believe miracles can have no natural explanation should refrain from defining miracles as divine violations of natural laws and simply define them rather as permanently inexplicable direct acts of God. Severe epistemological problems, as we will see, remain. But to define the miraculous in this sense captures the basic theistic intent while avoiding most of the traditional conceptual problems.

Not all philosophers and theologians, however, maintain that a direct act of God must be inexplicable scientifically to be considered miraculous. Consider, for example, the following illustration by R. F. Holland:

> A child riding his toy motor-car strays on to an unguarded railway crossing near his house and a wheel of his car gets stuck down the side of one of the rails. An express train is due to pass with the signals in its favour and a curve in the track makes it impossible for the driver to stop his train in time to avoid any obstruction he might encounter on the crossing. The mother coming out of the house to look for her child sees him on the crossing and hears the train approaching. She runs forward shouting and waving. The little boy remains seated in his car looking downward, engrossed in the task of pedalling it free. The brakes of the train are applied and it comes to rest a few feet from the child. The mother thanks God for the miracle; which she never ceases to think of as such although, as she in due course learns, there was nothing supernatural about the manner in which the brakes of the train came to be applied. The driver had fainted, for a reason that had nothing to do with the presence of the child on the line, and the brakes were applied automatically as his hand ceased to exert pressure on the control lever.

The event sequence described in this situation includes no observable component for which an empirical (natural) explanation for the event type in question is not available. It is quite normal for boys to play on train tracks and for engineers to faint and for the brakes to be applied when an engineer's hand releases the control lever. But the fact that the engineer fainted at precisely the moment necessary to save the child's life is quite extraordinary. And in the minds of some philosophers and theologians, coincidences such as this—assuming that they are also direct acts of God—can also be labeled miraculous. For the event sequencing in such cases is so extraordinary, they argue, that such events are just as awe-producing as those direct acts of God for which the event types in question cannot be given a natural explanation and, thus, have just as much right to be considered miraculous.

There is a radically subjective aspect of such 'coincidence miracles' which must be explicitly emphasized. The proponent of 'coincidence miracles' argues that explicable direct acts of God can be considered miraculous if they, like the events in Holland's train story, contain event sequencing which is extraordinary or awe-producing. But exactly how awe-producing must such event sequencing be? Consider, for example, the following two situations:

> Case A: June, a college student, will soon be dismissed from school if she fails to pay a $500 debt. She feels very strongly, however, that God wishes her to remain in school and, therefore, asks God to verify her 'call' by providing her with the necessary funds. A few days later, June receives a letter from a

> distant aunt with whom she has not corresponded for years. The aunt writes that, while praying a few days earlier, she had suddenly felt that June might be in need of financial assistance. Accordingly, the letter continues, she is enclosing a check for $500.
>
> Case B: Bill, a young father of three, has been unable to find employment for months. Finally, believing in the 'power of prayer', he asks for divine assistance in finding employment. Feeling quite confident, Bill eagerly looks through the 'help wanted' ads the next day. Much to his delight, he immediately discovers an interesting, applicable job advertisement. And upon responding to the advertisement, he is immediately hired.

Case A is somewhat striking. Students frequently need funds and relatives frequently furnish them. But the fact that a distant relative unknowingly gives just the right amount at the right time is highly unusual. Is it unusual enough, though, to be considered a candidate for the miraculous? And what of Case B? It is obviously not as unusual or extraordinary as the 'train story' or Case A. But is it unusual enough to be considered a candidate for the miraculous? Unfortunately, proponents of 'coincidence miracles' give us little guidance at this point. They often agree on a few paradigmatic 'text cases'. But enough significant disagreements arise to make it appear that the decision as to whether a given event is extraordinary enough to be labeled miraculous is quite relative—relative to the psychological perspective of each individual or group making the judgment.

Such epistemological subjectivity, we shall see later, has important epistemological and apologetical implications. But subjectivity of this sort does not make a concept incoherent. Thus 'coincidence miracle' remains a meaningful designation.

Some philosophers, however, question the intentions of those theists who do not define the miraculous as a scientifically inexplicable event. Flew, for example, strongly implies that such theists can rightly be accused of "simply changing the subject" to salvage their belief systems from incoherence or embarrassment.[10] But such criticism appears misguided. It may be true that some theists have given up defining 'miracle' in terms of inexplicability to avoid the scientific/philosophical problems it generates. But it is simply false to assume that this is always or even normally the case. Some of those theists who reject an inexplicability concept of miracle do so because they see it as inconsistent with the concept of (human) freedom they affirm. Others, on literary grounds, argue that the discussion of seemingly inexplicable events in the biblical text were never intended to be taken literally. And still others have no interest in an objective scientific analysis of the miraculous because they believe that divine activity is only to the 'eyes of faith'.

In short, the fact that some theists do not define the miraculous in terms of inexplicability is best seen not as their 'last ditch effort' to defend the miraculous against conceptual incoherence but as their attempt to affirm a concept of miracle which is compatible with their general theological systems.

Miracles as 'religiously significant events'

Some individuals maintain that a miracle must be more than an unusual event caused by God. Swinburne, for example, argues that a miracle must also have religious signifiance:

> If a god intervened in the natural order to make a feather land here rather than there for no deep ultimate purpose, or to upset a child's box of toys just for spite, these events would not naturally be described as miracles. To be a miracle an event must contribute significantly towards a holy divine purpose for the world . . . Extraordinary events lacking religious significance are more appropriately characterized as magical or physic phenomena rather than as miracles.[11]

One aspect of this line of reasoning seems acceptable. Many theists believe that they know enough about God and his creative purposes to know that certain types of events ought never be viewed as the result of direct divine activity—e.g., brutal torture, mass starvation, mass genocide or lingering painful deaths. Such events, they argue, must always be seen as either an unavoidable by-product of a world in which God has given us meaningful freedom or the product of malevolent forces.

But most classical Christian theists deny that we can accurately assess God's causal relationship to all that we experience. Since we do not have the ability to always determine correctly whether an occurrence is purposeful or just, we cannot, they acknowledge, *always* correctly assume that an event which appears to be nonpurposeful or capricious actually is and, thus, could not have been directly caused by God. And since malevolent agents such as Satan can perform activities which appear to us to be benevolent and purposeful, we cannot automatically assume that an event which appears to us to be just and purposeful actually is and, thus, can rightly be considered a candidate for direct divine causation.

It is questionable, therefore, whether Swinburne ought to consider 'religious significance' a third, independent definitional criterion. We can meaningfully discuss 'unusualness' apart from 'divine causation' and vice versa. But such is not always the case for 'religious significance'. For there appears to be no set of objective *independent* criteria by which the theist can determine in all cases whether an event contributes to some holy, just purpose. Rather, the theist may in some cases be able to declare that an event contributes to a holy purpose only *after* she has determined that it has been caused by God.

Or, stated differently, Swinburne is right to say that only those divinely caused extraordinary events which have religious significance are usually considered miraculous. But the decision as to whether any given event has religious significance is not always a third decision which is made in addition to those concerning 'unusualness' and 'divine causation'. Rather, in some cases, it is only because an extraordinary event is believed to have been caused by God that it is assumed to have religious significance. Accordingly, it seems best to us not to include 'religious significance' as a distinct, primary definitional criterion for miracle.

Conclusion

We have found then that there are two conceptually acceptable definitional readings for the miraculous: (1) a permanently inexplicable event directly caused by God and (2) an awe-producing naturally explicable event directly caused by God. Both are coherent, and together they seem to capture what the majority of theists have in mind when they use the term 'miracle' today. However, most contemporary philosophical discussion of the miraculous concentrate on issues related to (1). Thus, since the purpose of this book is to analyze the relationship between contemporary philosophy and 'miracle', we shall do the same.

NOTES

[1]See, for example, Patrick Nowell-Smith, "Miracles - The Philosophical Approach," *Hibbert Journal* 48 (June, 1950): 354-60.

[2]David Hume, *Enguires Concerning the Human Understanding and Concerning the Principles of Morals*, 2nd ed., edited by L. A. Selby-Bigge (Oxford:Clarendon Press, 1972), pp. 109-31.

[3]Alistair McKinnon, " 'Miracle' and 'Paradox', *American Philosophical Quarterly* 4 (October, 1967): 309-12.

[4]Antony Flew, "Parapsychology Revisited: Laws, Miracles and Repeatability," *The Humanist* 36 (May/June, 1976): 28-30.

[5]See, for example, Richard Swinburne, *The Concept of Miracle* (London:Macmillan, 1970, pp. 29-32; Peter Byrne, "Miracles and the Philosophy of Science," Heythrop Journal (April, 1978): 166-69; Grace Jantzen, "Hume on Miracles, History and Politics," *Christian Scholar's Review* 8 (1978): 322; J. Kellenberger, "Miracles," *International Journal for Philosphy of Religion* 10 (1979): 152-53.

[6]Doug Odegard, "Miracles and Good Evidence," *Religious Studies* 18 (1982): 37.

[7]Swinburne, pp. 29-32.

[8]For a discussion of why it is important to speak of event types rather than event tokens in this context, see Chapter III, pp. 69-70.

[9]R. F. Holland, "The Miraculous," *American Philosophical Quarterly*, 2 (1965): 43.

[10]Antony Flew, "Miracles" *Encyclopedia of Philosophy*, 1972 ed., vol. 5, p. 353.

[11]Swinburne, pp. 8-9.

SELECTED BIBLIOGRAPHY

Chapter I

Basinger, David. "Miracles as Violations: Some Clarifications." *The Southern Journal of Philosophy* 22 (1984): 1-7.

Diamond, Malcolm. "Miracles." *Religious Studies* 9 (September, 1973): 307-24.

Dietl, Paul. "On Miracles." *American Philosophical Quarterly* 5 (April, 1968): 130-34.

Flew, Antony. *Hume's Philosophy of Belief*. New York: Humanities Press, 1961, pp. 173-213.

Flew, Antony. "Parapsychology Revisited: Laws, Miracles and Repeatability." *The Humanist* 36 (May/June, 1976): 28-30.

Geisler, Norman. *Miracles and Modern Thought*. Grand Rapids: Zondervan, 1982.

Holland, R.F. "The Miraculous." *American Philosophical Quarterly* 2 (January, 1965): 43-49.

Jantzen, Grace. "Hume of Miracles, History and Politics." *Christian Scholar's Review* 8 (1979): 318-25.

Kellenberger, J. "Miracles." *International Journal for Philosophy of Religion* 10 (1979): 145-62.

Lewis, C.S. *Miracles*, revised ed. London: Collins, Fontana Books, 1960, pp. 51, 63-64.

McKinnon, Alistair. " 'Miracles' and 'Paradox'." *American Philosophical Quarterly* 4 (October, 1967): 308-14.

Miles, T.R. "On Excluding the Supernatural." *Religious Studies* 10 (April, 1966): 141-50.

Nowell-Smith, Patrick. "Miracles—The Philosophical Approach." *Hibbert Journal* 48 (June, 1950): 354-60.

Odegard, Douglas. "Miracles and Good Evidence." *Religious Studies* 18 (1982): 37-46.

Robinson, Guy. "Miracles." *Ratio* 9 (December, 1967): 155-66.

Swinburne, Richard. *The Concept of Miracle*. London: Macmillan, 1970, pp. 1-11.

Walker, Ian. "Miracles and Violations." *International Journal for Philosophy of Religion* 13 (1982): 103-08.

Wallace, R.C. "Hume, Flew and the Miraculous." *The Philosophical Quarterly* 20 (July, 1970): 230-40.

Wie, Tan Tai. "Recent Discussions on Miracles." *Sophia* 9 (October, 1970): 21-28.

Young, Robert. "Miracles and Physical Impossibility." *Sophia* 11 (October, 1972): 29-35.

CHAPTER II

Can History Rule Out the Miraculous?

II
CAN HISTORY RULE OUT THE MIRACULOUS?

We have found that for the purposes of our discussion it is best to define the miraculous as a permanently inexplicable event directly caused by God. But could miracles of this sort ever be identified? Or, to ask the question a little more formally, are there certain events which are such that if they were to occur, we could justifiably maintain that they were miracles? An adequate response to this epistemological question requires the consideration of three more specific questions:

(1) Did the event in question actually occur as reported?

(2) Is the event actually permanently inexplicable?

(3) Was the event actually caused by God?

(1) is primarily a historical question, (2) is primarily a scientific question and (3) is primarily metaphysical/theological in nature. This chapter will concentrate on (1).

I

The obvious starting point in any discussion of the relation between miracles (unexplained events) and history is Hume's famous essay, "On Miracles."[1] It would certainly be of intrinsic value to engage in a detailed exposition and analysis of Hume's argument. But it will better serve the purposes of this chapter to use Hume's criticism of the miraculous as a starting point, or catalyst, in locating the significant epistemological issues and problems which arise as the contemporary historian faces events allegedly contrary to accepted laws of nature.

Hume's first task in "On Miracles" is to remind us of his famous epistemological maxim: Experience is our only guide in reasoning concerning matters of fact. Or to be more specific, he reminds us that the constant conjunctions found in our past experience are our only guides in relation to experiential matters. From this maxim, we are told, two, more specific, epistemological principles follow. First, it follows that, when deciding whether to believe that a given event has actually occurred, the wise man must proportion his belief to the experiential evidence at hand. If the given type of event under consideration has always occurred conjoined with the type of situation in which it is found, then the wise man "expects the event with the last degree of assurance and regards his past experience as a full proof of the future existence of that event."[2] But if the given type of event under consideration has not always occurred conjoined with the type of situation in which it is found (or possibly has seldom or never occurred in one's past experience at all), things become more complicated. The wise man must then, Hume asserts, weigh the evidence—the amount of past experience on both sides of this issue—and place his belief on the side with the superior weight or probability.

Second, it also follows from his general epistemological maxim, Hume adds, that when assessing the testimony of human witnesses, the wise man must proportion his belief to the conjunctive relationship existing between a witness' past testimony and true states of affairs. If a given witness has proven extremely reliable in his past testimony, his present testimony warrants belief. But, if such a witness, upon occasion, has offered false testimony in the past, we are only justified in giving credence to any present testimony in proportion to the 'truth probability ratio' such a witness has established.

With these specific principles on which to build, Hume generates his major criticism of the miraculous. A miracle, he tells us, is a violation of a natural law by a god or some invisible agent. But natural laws are actually nothing more than those empirical regularities which summarize our unaltered, uniform past experience with certain types of natural phenomena. Thus, every miracle is automatically in direct opposition to our uniform past experience. But, in relation to the actual occurrence of events, he reminds us, uniform experience amounts to a proof. Thus, we must conclude that "from the very nature of the fact"—i.e., because of the uniform experience against every miraculous claim—the proof against a miracle "is as entire as any argument from experience can possibly imagine."[3]

The only reason we ever have for doubting this proof from "the very nature of the fact," Hume quickly adds, is the testimony of witnesses who claim to have observed an event in direct opposition to our uniform past experience.[4] And some such witnesses, he is willing to grant, may have proved extremely reliable in the past. But in weighing the evidence from "the very nature of the fact" against the evidence from human testimony," it is more probable that the [witness] should either deceive or be deceived [than] that the fact which he related should really have happened."[5] And, accordingly, we must conclude, he tells us, that "no testimony is sufficient to establish the occurrence of a miracle", except in the extremely improbable situation where "the falsehood of [the witness'] testimony would be more miraculous than the event which he relates. Then and not till then can he pretend to command [our] belief or opinion."[6]

Hume, however, is still somewhat dissatisfied. He has allowed for the bare, logical possibility that enough testimony could be given to establish belief in a miracle, and even this concession is too liberal for him. He sets out, accordingly, to establish that "there never was a miraculous event established on so full evidence."[7]

First of all, he tells us, no miracle has ever been attested to by enough men with enough learning to "secure against delusion" or enough integrity "to place them beyond all suspicion of any design to deceive others."[8] Second, experience teaches that men have a passion for surprise and wonder and, therefore, have the tendency to readily believe in miraculous events. Third, experience shows that stories and testimonies concerning the miraculous chiefly abound among ignorant and barbarous nations. And finally, he argues, different religions testify to the miraculous as an authentication to their truth. Thus, testimony given to establish different conflicting religions mutually destroys itself.

"It appears," consequently, he concludes, "that no testimony for any kind of miracle has ever amounted to a probability, much less a proof."[9] And we can, thus, safely "establish it as a maxim that no human testimony can have such force as to prove a miracle, and make it a just foundation for any such system of religion."[10]

Hume's remarks have been subject to various interpretations. Some have argued that he is attempting to rule out, *a priori*, the possibility of miracles. That is, they claim that Hume is arguing that the occurrence of a miracle is logically impossible. But it is doubtful that this is what he has in mind. For as Hume, himself, taught us, events which are contrary to our ordinary or previously uniform past experience are "intelligible and can be distinctly conceived." And "whatever is intelligible and can be distinctly conceived implies no contradiction, and can never be proved false by any demonstration, or abstract reasoning *a priori*."[11]

But if Hume is not claiming that miracles *cannot* occur, what then is he saying? It seems best to assume he is making an epistemological contention. That is, he seems to be arguing that we never have enough evidence to establish that the miraculous has occurred. But this claim ought not be seen as strictly *a posteriori* in nature. That is, he is not simply saying that there has *never yet* been enough historical evidence to establish a miracle, although this might someday be the case. Hume is arguing that the wise man will *never* find the singular, unverifiable nature of pro-miraculous human testimony to outweigh the verifiable, public, uniform nature of the relevant anti-miraculous evidence. He is, in short, making an *a priori* statement about the nature of all possible evidence—past, present and future. We will, he is arguing, never have an adequate epistemological basis for *believing* that a miracle (as an unexplained event) has occurred.

II

The leading contemporary proponent of this Humean perspective is Antony Flew. And since Flew not only defends Hume's argument (in contemporary terminology) but strengthens it, it is with Flew's line of reasoning which we will be concerned. In its basic form, Flew's argument runs as follows:

(4) It is the duty of the historian "to reconstruct what actually happened in the past by interpreting the present detritus of the past as historical evidence."[12]

(5) This detritus—documents, ruins, etc.—can be interpreted by the historian as evidence "only and precisely by appealing to what he knows or thinks he knows about how things in fact happen in the world, what is in fact probable or improbable and what is in fact possible or impossible."[13]

(6) Laws of nature (nomologicals) express the scientist's (and thus the historian's) current understanding of what is possible or impossible. Such laws "assert not that something is logically necessary or logically impossible (inconceivable) but that it is in fact necessary or in fact impossible."[14]

(7) Accordingly, if a purported historical event is inconsistent with current nomologicals, we must assume either that such nomologicals are inadequate or that the event did not occur as reported.

(8) But, the report of the alleged counterinstance is by its very nature only expressible by a singular, past tense, untestable proposition while the relevant nomologicals are expressed by "universal proposition which . . . have been and still can be tested, given certain conditions, anywhere at any time."[15]

(9) The historian must proportion his belief to the evidence.

(10) Thus, if a purported historical event is inconsistent with current nomologicals, the historian "cannot possibly know, on historical evidence, that it did so happen."[16] Its occurrence, rather, must be ruled physically impossible.

It is important to emphasize that this argument applies to *any* event which is purportedly inconsistent with current nomologicals, not just to those alleged counterinstances which some individuals also consider to be miraculous. To fail to keep this in mind can cause us inadvertently to allow controversial, but presently irrelevant, issues related to concepts such as 'violation' or 'divine causation' to creep into the discussion of (4-10). Neither Flew nor some of his critics are always as careful in this regard as they should be.

But quite apart from this fact, there has been a great deal of confusion concerning what Flew is actually arguing here. Part of the problem stems from the misleading reading of (10) Flew initially gave in *Hume's Philosophy of Belief*:

> Finding what appears to be historical evidence for an occurrence inconsistent with such a nomological, we must always insist on interpreting the evidence in some other way: For if the nomological is true then it is physically impossible that any event incompatible with it would have occurred.[17]

Some have concluded on the basis of this statement that the purpose of (4-10) is to make an ontological claim: that the historian can legitimately conclude that events which conflict with current nomologicals did not, in fact, occur as reported. Flew, however, explicitly informs us in other passages that this is not what he is saying. He acknowledges that some events inconsistent with our present laws might have occurred as reported. His argument, as (10) makes clear, is epistemological. He is arguing that, given the nature of the releveant historical evidence available, the historian could never have better reasons (a more justifiable evidential basis) for believing that an alleged counterinstance to a current nomological has occurred than for believing (and thus ruling) that it did not.

Another common complaint is that (4-10) rules out the possibility of scientific progress. If any alleged event which is inconsistent with current nomologicals must be considered physically impossible, is it not the case that all nomologicals and, thus, the body of scientific knowledge as a whole, are immune from change?

As we shall see later, this type of criticism is not totally misguided. But in its present form it fails. Flew readily admits that we do not have the ability to identify *true* nomologicals. In fact, he criticizes Hume for taking "for granted that what in his day he and all his fellow men of sense firmly believed about the order of nature constituted not just humanly fallible opinion, but the incorrigible last word" and for failing "to appreciate that (nomologicals) are themselves subject to criticism and correction."[18] Accordingly, Flew is quite willing to admit that new evidence—e.g., undeniable counterexamples—might emerge which would force us to discard or modify a current nomological and, thus, reassess the historicity of any alleged occurrence which, on the basis of this nomological, had previously been ruled physically impossible. He argues, for example, that although Herodotus was justified, given the astronomical and geographical nomologicals of his day, in labeling as untrue the claims of certain Phoenician sailors concerning unusual movements of the sun, updated nomologicals now make these claims quite plausible.

But has not Flew here trapped himself? He acknowledges that current nomologicals must be revised when the natural scientist is confronted "with some occurrence inconsistent with the proposition previously believed to express a law of nature."[19] Given (4-10), however, upon what basis could a scientist ever justifiably claim that such a counterinstance had in fact occurred as reported? Given (4-10), must not the scientist in the case of every alleged counterinstance weigh the singular, past tense proposition describing the counterinstance against the universal, present tense, testable propositions describing the relevant nomologicals and rule in favor of the latter?

In other words, it appears that Flew is caught in a dilemma. In (4-10), he seems to argue that the scientist (or historian) can only justifiably claim that a purported event has in fact occurred if such an event is consistent with current nomologicals. But it would seem that by his own admission some events which appear inconsistent with current nomologicals cannot be ruled out in this fashion, for it is only the acknowledged occurrence of a 'true' counterinstance which Flew believes can justifiably cause us to revise the current nomologicals in question. Or, stated somewhat differently yet, the dilemma is this. In (4-10) Flew seems to argue that the 'occurrence status' of all events is to be determined by (is dependent on) their consistency with current nomologicals. But it appears that he can only affirm the revisability of such nomologicals if he grants that the 'occurrence status' of some alleged counterinstances can be established independently of (separately from) the nomological(s) with which they are purportedly inconsistent.

To evaluate this criticism, it is necessary to discuss in greater detail Flew's understanding of nomological revisability. Flew concedes that if the testimonial evidence for an alleged counterinstance seems extremely strong, "then perhaps the historian may ask himself whether the nomological proposition that precludes the event is after all true. It could, in principle at least, be further tested."[20] But the key to such testing, Flew emphasizes, is repeatability. "The whole object of the scientific exercise is to discover true laws, and theories that explain the truth of these laws. If alleged phenomena are not repeatable at all, then they clearly cannot be subsumed under any natural law."[21] In such cases, Flew maintains, "it could still be that the event did occur. Yet... no matter how impressive the testimony might appear, the most favorable verdict that history could ever return must be the agnostic and appropriately Scottish 'not proven'."[22]

In short, Flew denies that the revision of a nomological requires that the scientist accept the actual occurrence of any single alleged counterinstance before the revision is made. It is, he argues, only when an event (E) which appears to be a counterinstance to a given nomological is shown to be repeatable that the scientist can justifiably content that E, as an event token, actually occurred as reported and is, thus, required to search for a revised or new nomological under which it can be subsumed.

It is, therefore, inaccurate to assume that Flew is in some obvious sense contradicting himself by affirming both (4-10) and the revisability of current nomologicals. In (4-10) Flew is arguing that the evidence for a particular historical (or contemporary) event could never, by itself, force us to acknowledge that such an event has actually occurred and, thus, that the relevant nomological must be revised. Such a contention is not inconsistent with Flew's claim that a seeming counterinstance could initiate the revision of a nomological. For he also holds that it is only if a counterinstance can be shown to be repeatable that a revision must be sought, and of course it requires more than singular, past tense evidence supporting any given event token to establish repeatability.

Finally, it is sometimes argued that (4-10) demonstrates an arbitrary and dogmatic naturalistic prejudice on the part of Flew. What right, it is argued, does Flew have to assume that the laws of science have the ultimate say in relation to history? How can other, nonnaturalistic factors be automatically ruled out?

This criticism is also misguided. Flew repeatedly emphasizes that he is, in the context of (4-10), only discussing what the historian can conclude on the basis of the historical (natural) evidence alone. He is not at this point, he tells us, attempting to rule out the possibility that the historicity of certain events could be established on the basis of nonnatural criteria—e.g., some form of revelation from God.[23]

Moreover, his decision to consider only 'natural' historical criteria cannot in this context be considered arbitrary. He does so because he is assuming that theists wish to use miracles to help establish or support religious belief. And he rightly sees that an alleged miracle can only have this apologetical value if its occurrence can be established on 'natural' grounds.

There are, however, serious problems with (4-10). Flew argues that unless an alleged counterinstance to a current nomological is repeatable, the historian cannot justifiably rule that the event has occurred as reported. But let us assume, for example, that a large group of internationally renowned physicians report that they have all observed a severely deformed and withered leg instantaneously return to its normal size and shape. Such an occurrence would obviously be inconsistent with well-established current nomologicals. Thus, given Flew's 'occurrence criterion', those of us who heard this claim could not affirm that this event had actually occurred as reported until it could be repeated—i.e., until events of the same type could be produced. In fact, given Flew's 'occurrence criterion', even the doctors, themselves, would be forced to withhold affirmation until repeatibility was demonstrated.

Such reasoning, however, is problematic. The problem is not that Flew wants us to proportion our belief to the evidence. The problem is Flew's contention that the evidence supporting our current nomologicals—e.g., the evidence supporting our belief that deformed, withered legs do not return instantly to healthy state—should *always* be considered to outweight all the other forms of evidence which might support the occurrence of a nonrepeatable counterinstance to such nomologicals—e.g., the testimonies of renowned physicians who understand the relevant physiological laws. Flew bases this contention, remember, on his belief that nomologicals are expressed by "universal propositions which . . . have been and still can be tested, given certain conditions, anywhere at any time" while the report of any alleged counterinstance is by its very nature only expressible by a singular, past tense, untestable proposition. But such a comparison is misguided.

Flew is certainly correct to argue that nomologicals are expressed by universal propositions which have been and can still be thoroughly tested, and, thus, we certainly are justified in using such nomologicals to predict in general what will or will not occur under certain conditions. We do, for example, have well-established nomologicals which state (or imply) that withered legs do not instantly return to a normal condition, and, thus, we should not expect such occurrences. However, Flew's claim that reports of nonrepeatable counterinstances to such nomologicals are always singular, past tense, untestable propositions is deceptive. It is, of course, true that no past occurrence can, itself, be repeated or reobserved directly. And it is generally true that a report which claims that such an occurrence was a counterinstance to current nomologicals will be expressed by a singular, past tense proposition. However, the trustworthiness of our apparent memories of the past and the trustworthiness of the reports of others about their memories of the past are not 'past tense', untestable issues.

Consider, for example, the widely accepted epistemological principle which states that when we are fully awake, are in a healthy psychological state, have healthy visual apparatus and are consciously concentrating upon that which we are looking, what we are observing is generally what others would observe under these conditions and, thus, our observations can be considered reliable. This principle is not a past tense, singular, nontestable proposition. It is a testable generalization which is continually reaffirmed in formal and informal settings. Or consider the widely accepted epistemological principle which states that if different individuals who have no vested interest in the occurrence of a given state of affairs independently experience the 'same' phenomenon at the same time in the same setting under normal conditions, what they claim to have observed can generally be accepted as having occurred. This is also a present tense generalization which is continually being reaffirmed in formal and informal settings.

In fact, some 'observation-confirming' principles of this sort must be affirmed by anyone who wishes to affirm the acceptability of any given nomological for, as Flew himself acknowledges, nomologicals are, in their most basic sense, descriptive generalizations which summarize the *reported observations* of individuals (or groups of individuals).

Accordingly, if a group of renowned physicians were to report that they have observed a withered leg restored instantly to a healthy state, we would not, as Flew implies, have a simple conflict between our current, testable, present tense nomologicals and a singular, past tense, untestable report. We would have a conflict between our current, testable, present tense nomologicals and our current, testable, present tense observation-confirming (testimonial) principles.

Now, of course, seemingly trustworthy observation reports can be mistaken. We all at times misperceive or miscommunicate what we accurately perceive. It is possible, for example, that the physicians in our scenario were victims of an elaborate hoax or that they have intended to deceive us for some unknown reason or that their observation report has been misinterpreted or miscommunicated. Moreover, the fact that an occurrence report—e.g., the claim that a withered leg returned instantly to a normal state—is incompatible with well-established nomologicals is, of course, a good reason to suspect misperception or miscommunication. Accordingly, given the scenario under consideration, those of us who heard the physicians's claim would have to convince ourselves that we had not been deceived or that the report had not been miscommunicated or misunderstood. Even the physicians would have to convince themselves they had not been deceived in some manner.

But as Flew, himself, admits, nomologicals are corrigible; they have and will continue to be revised or discarded. And as Flew also admits, some occurrence reports which were, at the time they were initially made, incompatible with well-established nomologicals, and, thus, doubted are now accepted as accurate. Therefore, there appears to be no strong *a priori* basis for refusing to acknowledge the accuracy of occurrence reports which challenge our current nomologicals. We do in *all* such cases have the *prima facie* evidence of the general, present tense, testable nomologicals which counts against the reliability (accuracy) of the occurrence report. But we may in some such cases also have the *prima facie* evidence of well-entrenched, general, present tense, testable observation-confirming principles which supports the reliability of the occurrence report. And Flew has given us no objective basis for maintaining that the evidence from well-entrenched, testable nomologicals should *always* outweigh the evidence from well-entrenched, testable observation-confirming (testimonial) principles.

Moreover, as Swinburne rightly points out, we do not have only the evidence from observation reports and relevant nomologicals to consider. We must also consider any relevant physical traces—i.e., presently observable empirical data which indicates that some specific phenomenon has occurred in the past.[24] In the scenario under discussion, relevant physical traces might be x-rays (or photographs) of the leg taken just before and just after the alleged 'healing'. An even more compelling physical trace would be a videotape of the incident. Now, of course, x-rays, photographs and videotapes can be altered and, thus, such physical traces could not establish conclusively that the event had actually occurred as reported. And since the traces would in this case be incompatible with well-established nomologicals, we would need to be suspicious. But we have generally accepted methods for assessing (testing) the accurance of x-rays, photographs and videotapes. And if it proved highly probable that they were reliable, such data would obviously stand as very strong evidence for the accuracy of the occurrence report in question.

But exactly how much 'testimonial' and/or 'physical' evidence can justifiably be said to outweigh the evidence against such an occurrence furnished by the relevant nomologicals? This is not an easy question to answer. It seems to us, though, that certain general assessment principles can be affirmed with some conviction. It seems reasonable, for example, to maintain that if we only read reports of alleged counterinstances in the newspaper or 'history books' or if none of the individuals directly involved is still alive and/or if the report is given to support some system to which the 'witness' is committed, we ought initially to be suspicious and require more information before affirming the accuracy of the report. It seems reasonable to hold in fact that apart from those cases in which those who claim to have observed supposed counterinstances can be directly interviewed and investigated or in which there are widely accepted compelling physical traces, we ought to at best suspend judgment with respect to the accuracy of such reports. But let us assume that we, ourselves, directly observe a counterinstance under normal conditions and can discover no hoax. Or let us assume that we can verify directly that knowledgeable, reputable individuals have claimed to have observed a counterinstance and can also verify that such individuals have no vested interest in making such a claim and that there has been no hoax. Or let us assume that we have very reliable physical traces related to a seeming counterinstance—e.g., reliable videotapes of the event. Under such conditions, it would clearly be quite reasonable to assume at least tentatively that the event has indeed occurred as reported.

It appears, then, to summarize our critique of (4-10), that Flew's major problem is his *overemphasis* on the importance of repeatability. He is right to argue that scientific laws are immune from change until we can produce *repeatable* counterinstances to them. But he is wrong to contend that a seeming counterinstance must be repeatable before we can justifiably contend that it has occurred. Since nonrepeatable counterinstances, as well as the relevant laws, can be supported by general, testable principles, there is, at least in principle, a point at which it would no longer be reasonable to deny that certain nonrepeatable counterinstances have taken place.

Moreover, this flaw in Flew's line of reasoning should not be seen as irrelevant to the scientific enterprise. (4-10) does not rule out scientific progress since Flew does allow for change in scientific theories once a counterinstance has been shown to be repeatable. But if the scientist must always assume that any seeming counterinstance did not occur *until* it can be shown to be repeatable, he or she may be much less likely to take reports of seeming counterinstances seriously and, thus, less likely to attempt to demonstrate repeatability. And this could, indeed, have a negative impact on the rate at which scientific progress is made.

It might be argued in response that although there are, in principle, certain types of evidence which would make it most reasonable for the scientist or historian to affirm the occurrence of a nonrepeatable counterinstance, there has never in actuality been compelling evidence of this sort and, thus, that Flew's 'occurrence criterion' is, as a scientific or historical tool for assessing actual occurrences, acceptable.

But to argue in this fashion is unacceptable on two counts. First, unless we beg the question at hand by assuming that no amount of evidence can outweigh the fact that an occurrence is a counterinstance to a well-established nomological, there is little reason to grant that individuals have never in fact had sufficient evidence for believing that such counterinstances have occurred. Those, for example, who observed counterinstances to Ptolemaic theories certainly had sufficient evidence for accepting their observations, even before such observations were shown to be repeatable. But, more importantly, to argue in this fashion misses the point of Flew's argument. Flew is not simply claiming that there has never in fact been compelling evidence for affirming the occurrence of a nonrepeatable counterinstance. His claim is that there could *in fact* never be such evidence. Thus, even if no such counterinstance has been established in the past, this would in no sense establish that compatibility with current nomologicals ought, as

Flew believes, to be considered an *a priori*, necessary 'occurrence criterion' for the historian. We would still, in each case we encounter, need to assess the evidence at hand.

To be fair to Flew, though, we must reemphasize his belief that we cannot affirm simultaniously both a nomological and an exception to it. Thus, for Flew to acknowledge, for example, that physicians have accurately reported the instantaneous healing of a withered leg would necessitate that the relevant nomological be rejected or modified. Hence, in order to preserve our well-entrenched, useful nomologicals, he considers a very strong 'occurrence criterion' necessary. But as was argued in the last chapter, unless a counterinstance is repeatable, it does not destroy the relevant nomological. And once this fact is understood, to acknowledge the occurrence of a nonrepeatable counterinstance becomes much less threatening and the need for a strong 'occurrence criterion' such as Flew's is, thus, greatly diminished.

Moreover, it must be reemphasized that we are at this point only talking about events which are incompatible with current nomologicals. We are not talking about *miracles*. Of course, if we must acknowledge that nonrepeatable counterinstances are, in principle, identifiable, then we cannot rule out the identifiability of those purportedly miraculous events which are incompatible with current nomologicals *solely* because of such incompatibility. But to acknowledge the occurrence of an event which is believed by some to be a miracle in no sense commits one to affirming that it is in fact miraculous. An acknowledged counterinstance must also be identifiable as a direct act of God and as a permanently inexplicable occurrence before it can justifiably be labeled miraculous.

Conclusion

We must conclude then that the historian cannot in an *a priori* manner rule that all reports of nonrepeatable counterinstances must be considered inaccurate. The fact that a reported occurrence is incompatible with well-established nomologicals does count strongly against the acceptability of the report. And it is not easy to say exactly how much evidence is needed to counterbalance such nomological evidence. But a decision concerning the acceptability of such occurrence reports must be made on a case by case basis.

NOTES

[1]David Hume, *Enquires Concerning the Human Understanding and Concerning the Principles of Morals*, 2nd ed., edited by L. A. Selby-Bigge (Oxford: Clarendon Press, 1972), pp. 109-31.

[2]Ibid., p. 110.

[3]Ibid., p. 116.

[4]Ibid.

[5]Ibid.

[6]Ibid.

[7]Ibid., pp. 116-127.

[8]Ibid., pp. 116-120.

[9]Ibid., p. 127.

[10]Ibid., p. 127.

[11]Ibid., p. 133.

[12]Antony Flew, "Parapsychology Revisited: Laws, Miracles and Repeatability," *The Humanist* 36 (May/June, 1976): 29.

[13]Ibid.

[14]Ibid.

[15]Ibid., p. 30.

[16]Ibid., p. 29.

[17]Antony Flew, *Hume's Philosophy of Belief* (New York: Humanities Press, 1961), p. 207.

[18]Antony Flew, "Miracles," *Encyclopedia of Philosophy*, 1972 ed., vol. 5, p. 351.

[19]Ibid.

[20]Ibid., p. 349.

[21]Ibid., p. 352.

[22]Flew, *The Humanist*, p. 30.

[23]Flew, *Encyclopedia*, p. 352.

[24]Richard Swinburne, *The Concept of Miracle* (London: Macmillan, 1970), pp. 33-50.

SELECTED BIBLIOGRAPHY

Chapter II

Basinger, David. "Flew, Miracles and History." *Sophia* 22 (July, 1983): 15-22.

Brown, Colin. *Miracles and the Critical Mind.* Grand Rapids: Eerdmans, 1983, pp. 171-97.

Clark, Gordon. "Miracles, History and Natural Law." *The Evangelical Quarterly* 12 (January, 1940).

Colwell, Gary. "Miracles and History." *Sophia* 22 (July, 1983): 9-14.

Colwell, Gary. "On Defining Away the Miraculous." *Philosophy* 57 (July, 1982): 327-37.

Flew, Antony. *Hume's Philosophy of Belief.* New York: Humanities Press, 1961, pp. 173-213.

Flew, Antony. "Parapsychology Revisited: Laws, Miracles and Repeatability." *The Humanist* 36 (May/June, 1976): 28-30.

Flew, Antony. "Miracles." *Encyclopedia of Philosophy*, 1972 ed., Vol. 5, pp. 346-53.

Geisler, Norman. *Miracles and Modern Thought.* Grand Rapids: Zondervan, 1982.

Hambourger, Robert. "Belief in Miracles and Hume's Essay." *Nous* 14 (1980): 587-604.

Hume, David. *Enquires Concerning the Human Understanding and Concerning the Principles of Morals*, 2d. Edited by L.A. Selby-Bigge. Oxford: Clarendon Press, 1972, pp. 109-31.

King-Farlow, John. "Historical Insights on Miracles: Babbage, Hume, Aquinas." *International Journal for Philosophy of Religion* 13 (1982): 209-18.

Sorenson, Roy A. "Hume's Scepticism Concerning Reports of Miracles." *Analysis* 43 (January, 1983): 60.

Swinburne, Richard. *The Concept of Miracle.* London: Macmillan, 1970, pp. 33-53.

Wallace, R.C. "Hume, Flew and the Miraculous." *The Philosophical Quarterly* 20 (July, 1970): 230-240.

Wertz, S.K. "Is Hume's Use of Evidence as Bad as Norton Says It Is?" *Philosophicals Topics*, Vols. 79-86, Supp. 80.

Young, Robert. "Miracles and Epistemology." *Religious Studies* 8 (June, 1972): 115-26.

CHAPTER III

Can Science Identify the Miraculous?

III

CAN SCIENCE IDENTIFY THE MIRACULOUS?

We are currently considering the question of whether miracles—if defined as inexplicable direct acts of God—can be indentified. This question, as we have noted, can only be answered by considering three more specific questions:

(1) Did the event in question actually occur as reported?

(2) Is the event permanently inexplicable scientifically?

(3) Was the event directly caused by God?

In Chapter II, we discussed (1), concluding that this question must be answered on a case by case basis. In this chapter, we shall consider (2).

I

What exactly does it mean to say that an event is permanently inexplicable scientifically? For example, what does it mean for a theist to claim that the resurrection of Jesus is a permanently inexplicable event? It does not mean simply that science *will never in fact* subsume this event under a covering law of some sort. This would be a rather weak claim since there is a large and somewhat unexciting class of events which are, in principle, explicable but which science will not in fact ever 'explain'—e.g., those events which have never been observed, some of those events never recorded, some of those *presently* inexplicable events not considered of great interest to scientists, etc.

To claim that an event is permanently inexplicable is to claim something much stronger. It is to claim that events such as the resurrection of Jesus *could never* be subsumed under any scientific covering law. But could we ever justifiably maintain that an event was permanently inexplicable in this sense?

The most common argument denying this possibility is stated well by Antony Flew:

(4) An event could only be labeled permanently inexplicable if we could justifiably state that it could never be subsumed under any nomological (covering law).

(5) But it is always possible that new information (scientific investigation) will force us to revise our current set of nomologicals related to any given type of occurrence.

(6) Therefore, we could never conclusively state with respect to any seemingly inexplicable event that it could never be subsumed under a revised or new nomological—i.e., we could never justifiably identify any given occurrence as permanently inexplicable.[1]

The crucial premise is (5). And many philosophers in addition to Flew see it as undeniable. Guy Robinson, for example, argues that we could only deny (5) if we were certain that the class of scientific theories was finite and that with respect to some event this class had within it no relevant, but as yet undiscovered, scientific theory to offer. But we have, he adds, absolutely no basis for maintaining that either of these contentions is true.[2]

Not all philosophers, however, agree. Such philosophers are not assuming they have complete and incorrigible knowledge of the natural order. Nor do they even assume that any specific nomological can ever justifiably be considered immune from revision. Their claim is weaker: that even granting that we might gather significant, new scientific data and greatly revise our current set of nomologicals accordingly, some conceivable events are such that, if they were to occur, we could justifiably rule that they could never be subsumed under a new or revised nomological.

But what are the criteria by which such permanently inexplicable events are to identified? The key, according to Richard Swinburne, lies in our ability (or inability) to devise new scientific laws to accommodate seemingly recalcitrant events. Let us assume that we encounter an event (E) which is a counterinstance to a law (L). If we can devise a new law (L!) which accommodates E and is simpler, coherent and yields new and more correct precictions than the current law (L) to which E is a counterinstance, then, Swinburne argues, we ought to replace L with L! (and, accordingly, no longer consider E a true counterinstance). But if there can be no new law (L') devised which accommodates E and is simpler, coherent and better able to yield successful predictions than the current law (L) to which E is a counterinstance, then E can justifiably be considered a nonrepeatable counterinstance. And nonrepeatable counterinstances, of course, cannot be subsumed under scientific covering laws.[3]

Now it is true, Swinburne acknowledges, that based on such a test, the 'repeatability status' of any given counterinstance is a corrigible matter. Hence some might doubt that we could ever decide with certainty that a counterinstance actually was inexplicable. But all claims to knowledge, he adds, are corrigible and we must reach provisional conclusions about them on the evidence available to us. Moreover, we have to some extent good evidence about what are the 'laws of nature', and some of them are so well-established and account for so many data that any modification of which we would suggest to account for the odd counterinstance would be so clumsy and *ad hoc* that it would upset the whole structure of science. For example, let us imagine that we experience the 'resurrection of . . . a man whose heart has not been beating for twenty-four hours and who was dead by other currently used criteria" or "water turning into wine without assistance of chemical apparatus or catalysts."[4] The relevant laws in such cases are well-entrenched; they cannot be modified or given up easily. Accordingly, he concludes, if such counterinstances were to occur, they could justifiably be considered violations of the laws of nature—i.e., permanently inexplicable events.

Margaret Boden argues in an analogous manner. She grants that observable phenomena cannot normally be dismissed as lying forever outside the range of science, but she is not convinced this would always have to be the case. For example, she argues, let us take the logically possible case of a leper whose missing fingers reappear instantly under the most stringent, fraud-detecting conditions—e.g., in the presence of doctors, TV cameras, etc. Such an event would conflict with so many well-established scientific facts that any attempt at revising our present scientific laws in such a way as to accommodate it would so weaken the predictive power of such laws that they would no longer be of practical value. Accordingly, she concludes, if such an event were actually to occur, the scientist, of necessity, would be forced to identify it as a permanently inexplicable phenomenon.[5]

Such reasoning has a *prima facie* appeal, but an obvious question arises. Swinburne and Boden freely acknowledge that the scientific enterprise is continually discovering new, often startling and unexpected, information about the causal relationships which operate in our universe. And they freely acknowledge that the annals of science record numerous instances in which supposed counterinstances to well-established scientific laws were later demonstrated—sometimes only after significant conceptual shifts—to in fact be consistent with such laws or revisions thereof. Accordingly, is it not the height of scientific provincialism for anyone to maintain solely on the basis of the data presently available that certain events could, if they were to occur, justifiably be labeled permanently inexplicable?

Swinburne and Boden obviously think not. And it is important to understand why. It is not, as was mentioned before, because they believe they have some privileged understanding of the 'true nature of reality'. It is rather that when faced with an acknowledged counterinstance to very well-established laws, they see only two options: to either modify the laws to accommodate the occurrence or affirm the adequacy of the laws and declare the event permanently inexplicable. And they feel that in many conceivable instances, the latter would be the more reasonable choice.

But is there not another opinion? Let us assume that after extensive testing, scientists cannot explain how water has turned into wine —i.e., cannot devise an explanation compatible with our current set of relevant laws. Why should we assume that they must then either radically modify such laws or declare the event permanently inexplicable? Why could they not continue to affirm the adequacy of our current set of laws and either continue to run further tests or label the occurrence a 'freak event' and await the occurrence of similar phenomena before seriously investigating further?

According to R. F. Holland, such a noncommital posture would place the relevant laws in a state of uncertainty and would therefore weaken the strength of the scientific method.[6] But such a response is unconvincing. For, as we have already seen (and as Swinburne explicitly acknowledges), only *repeatable* counterinstances falsify scientific laws. As long as a counterinstance—no matter how unusual—is not repeatable, we are presented with no competing hypothesis to challenge the current laws.

We must conclude, therefore, that the line of reasoning proposed by Swinburne and Boden is not acceptable. The major problem is not that its proponents assume too much about the 'true nature of reality'. The major problem is that it sets up a false dilemma. If, when faced with acknowledged counterinstances to well-established laws, we were forced to either modify or give up such laws or declare the counterinstances to be permanently inexplicable, the latter might well in some cases be the more reasonable choice. But this is not the only option to us. As long as seeming counterinstances are not repeatable, the scientist can (indeed should) continue to affirm the adequacy of the laws in question while continuing to search for new or modified laws to accommodate the recalcitrant events.

But perhaps there is another, slightly different way to defend the concept of permanent inexplicability. Not all defenders of this concept agree with Swinburne and Boden's claim that the scientific establishment itself can, in principle, identify permanently inexplicable events. They readily grant that the scientific enterprise should acknowledge no *a priori* explanatory limits in its quest to explain all observable phenomena. Thus, they grant that the *scientific establishment* ought never formally declare that an event could never be explained scientifically—i.e., they believe science ought always continue to search for a scientific explanation for all anomalies.

However, they argue, in our role as thoughtful individuals who consider and interpret the information furnished by the scientific enterprise, we know enough about the basic, well-established patterns of natural uniformity to be able to say with certainty that certain counterinstances to such laws could never be explained. For example, J. Kellenberger tells us, "We know enough about water to know that it physically cannot be turned into wine in the manner it was at Cana." And, "We know enough about death to know that a man cannot be brought back to life after being dead three days as Lazarus was."[7]

In short, their argument is that although we could never, in our role as scientists, label an event permanently inexplicable, we could, in our necessary role as 'metaphysical' observers of the scientific enterprise, justifiably determine that certain events should be given this designation.

But this line of reasoning is also unconvincing. Individuals such as Kellenberger might, themselves, be convinced that they know enough about the 'nature of reality' to identify certain conceivable events as permanently inexplicable. But why should we agree with them? They have given us no sound, objective basis for doing so. On the other hand, the annals of science do, as was mentioned before, record numerous instances in which counterinstances to supposedly well-established scientific laws were in fact demonstrated to be consistent with such laws or revisions thereof. Moreover, as was also mentioned before, there is no pragmatic need to determine whether a presently inexplicable (nonrepeatable) event is permanently inexplicable since nonrepeatable counterinstances do not damage the functional adequacy of the laws with which such anomalies are incompatible.

Accordingly, it seems to us that it would indeed be the height of metaphysical provincialism for anyone to maintain that all rational individuals ought to agree that certain events, if they were to occur, could never be explained by science. This is not to say, of course, that the types of events mentioned by Kellenberger and Swinburne would, if they were to occur, ever in fact be explained. Perhaps they would not. But it would always be more rational, we are arguing, to acknowledge our limited understanding of the nature of reality and, thus, assume that a scientific explanation may be forthcoming.

Some philosophical theists, however, will argue that we have overlooked an important relevant factor. They maintain that although our present inability to define the limits of scientific explicability does *normally* make it impossible to identify a given occurrence as permanently inexplicable, such is not the case if the occurrence in question is known to be a direct act of God. Douglas Erlandson, for example, tells us that:

> The believer may be quite willing to admit that the scientist has his autonomous province. There are many anomalous events which the scientist can investigate 'with impunity'. He contends, however, that certain events will remain forever beyond the province of scientific investigation and can give some indication which events they are ... When the events in question fit an appropriate (divine) pattern (which he can to some extent specify) they are miracles and will not be explained.[8]

And according to Grace Jantzen, it misses the point to consider only empirical factors when attempting to determine explicability:

> It is precisely when (an) irregular event ... if considered as divine intervention, would

> have enormous religious significance that there is reason to consider it miraculous and consequently permanently inexplicable by scientific methods: the two cannot be separated.[9]

In other words, it appears that some philosophers wish to support the indentifiability of permanently inexplicable events by arguing as follows:

(7) To say that a state of affairs (S) is a direct act of God is to say that direct divine influence is a necessary (and possibly sufficient) causal condition for the occurrence of S.

(8) Divine influence, by definition, is nonempirical, that is, can never be directly detected by the human senses or their extensions.

(9) Accordingly, any state of affairs (S) which has been identified as a direct act of God has at least one necessary causal factor which is nonempirical.

(10) But a scientific explanation for an event (E) is adequate (complete) only if it stipulates the necessity and sufficient conditions for the occurrence of E.

(11) Moreover, scientific explanations, by definition, stipulate only empirical causal factors.

(12) Therefore, it necessarily follows that if E is a direct act of God, it can never be given an adequate scientific explanation—i.e., it necessarily follows that E is a permanently inexplicable event.

There is, of course, a sense in which this line of reasoning is correct. If direct divine activity is in fact a necessary causal condition for a particular event (E) and if divine activity is considered nonempirical, then E cannot as an event token be given a scientific explanation.

But there is also an important sense in which such reasoning is misguided. As Swinburne and others have rightly pointed out, empirical science is not primarily interested in the causal nature of particular occurrences (event tokens). The objective of the empirical scientist rather is to map regularity patterns between certain types of phenomena and certain sets of antecedent causal conditions and then formulate such patterns into the general laws necessary for scientific explanation. That is to say, the scientist is generally interested in seeking explanations for event types as opposed to event tokens. For example, the birth of a particular baby is not considered scientifically explicable because scientists can offer an adequate explanation for this particular birth (as an event token) but because they can stipulate a set of empirical causal conditions under which birth (as an event type) can be explained. Or, to state this important point in a slightly different manner, the idea of a scientific explanation is more complicated than many people realize. What might not be scientifically inexplicable *as an event token* might at present or in the future be scientifically explicable *as an event type.*

Consequently, while the contention that all direct acts of God should be considered scientifically inexplicable is not strictly speaking false, it is very misleading. If an event (E) is a direct act of God, it is true that empirical science could never give a complete explanation for it as a particular event token. But, since to establish that an event is inexplicable as a event token does not demonstrate that it is not presently explicable or never will be explicable as an event type and since event type inexplicability is most significant for the scientific enterprise, knowing that God directly caused an event clearly does not establish alone that the event is scientifically inexplicable in its most important sense.

This same point can be made by returning to the notion of 'coincidence miracle' which was developed in Chapter 1. Christian theists often make a distinction between those 'miraculous' direct acts of God which are inexplicable scientifically—e.g., a healing—and those 'miraculous' direct acts of God which are awe-producing but explicable scientifically—e.g., the totally unexpected acquisition of a needed sum of money at the proper time. If this distinction is meaningful, then it obviously follows that knowing that an event is an act of God is not sufficient for knowing that the event is scientifically inexplicable. For since 'coincidence miracles' are by definition *scientifically explicable* direct acts of God, one can only claim that an event falls within this category if one denies that *all* direct acts of God are automatically beyond the limits of scientific explanation.

II

What we have argued in this chapter, it must be emphasized in closing, is not that miracles, defined as permanently inexplicable events, *do not* or *could not* occur. Nor have we argued that all actual or hypothetical events which are presently inexplicable will or even could be given scientific explanations. We have argued, though, that since there are no *a priori* limits to the explanatory power of the scientific enterprise and since anomalies do not destroy the usefulness of the relevant scientific laws, there could never exist a justifiable basis for maintaining at any given point in time that a given occurrence could never be given an adequate scientific explanation in the future. And, thus, we have concluded that miracles, if defined as permanently inexplicable events, could never justifiably be identified as such. Theists wishing to maintain that miracles are identifiable must either settle for 'present inexplicability' or drop any reference to scientific explicability altogether.

NOTES

[1]Antony Flew, "Miracles," *Encyclopedia of Philosophy*, 1972 ed., Vol. 5, pp. 348-49.

[2]Guy Robinson, "Miracles," *Ratio* 9 (December, 1967): 155-162.

[3]Richard Swinburne, *The Concept of Miracle* (London: Macmillan, 1970), pp. 29-32.

[4]Ibid., p. 32.

[5]Margaret Boden, "Miracles and Scientific Explanation," *Ratio* II (December, 1969): 137-41.

[6]R. F. Holland, "The Miraculous," *American Philosophical Quarterly* 2 (1965): 43-51.

[7]J. Kellenberger, "Miracles," *International Journal for Philosophy of Religion* 10 (1979): 153.

[8]Douglas Erlandson, "A New Look at Miracles," *Religious Studies* (December, 1977): 425.

[9]Grace Jantzen, "Hume on Miracles, History and Politics," *Christian Scholar's Review* 8 (1978): 325.

SELECTED BIBLIOGRAPHY

Chapter III

Basinger, David. "Christian Theism and the Concept of Miracle: Some Epistemological Perplexities." *The Southern Journal of Philosophy* 18 (1980): 137-50.

Basinger, David. "Miracles and Apologetics: A Response." *Christian Scholar's Review* 9 (1980): 348-53.

Basinger, David and Basinger, Randall. "Science and the Concept of Miracle." *Journal of the American Scientific Affiliation* 30 (December, 1978): 164-68.

Blackman, Larry. "The Logical Impossibility of Miracles in Hume." *International Journal for Philosophy of Religion* 9 (1978): 179-87.

Boden, Margaret. "Miracles and Scientific Explanation." *Ratio* 11 (December, 1969): 137-41.

Brown, Colin. *Miracles and the Critical Mind.* Grand Rapids: Eerdmans, 1983, pp. 197-239.

Byrne, Peter. "Miracles and the Philosophy of Science." *Heythrop Journal* (April, 1978): 162-70.

Erlandson, Douglas. "A New Look at Miracles." *Religious Studies* 15 (1979): 417-28.

Fern, Richard L. "Hume's Critique of Miracles: An Irrevelant Triumph." *Religious Studies* 18 (September, 1982): 337-54.

Flew, Antony. "Miracles." *Encyclopedia of Philosophy*, 1972 ed., Vol. 5, pp. 346-53.

Geisler, Norman. *Miracles and Modern Thought.* Grand Rapids: Zondervan, 1982.

Gill, John B. "Miracles With Method." *Sophia* 16 (October, 1977): 19-26.

Holland, R.F. "The Miraculous." *American Philosophical Quarterly* 2 (1965): 43-51.

Jantzen, Grace. "Hume on Miracles, History and Politics." *Christian Scholar's Review* 8 (1979): 318-25.

Kellenberger, J. "Miracles." *International Journal for Philosophy of Religion* 10 (1979): 145-62.

Pratt, Vernon. "The Inexplicable and the Supernatural." *Philosophy* 43 (July, 1968): 248-57.

Robinson, Guy. "Miracles." *Ratio* 9 (December, 1967): 155-66.

Schlesinger, George. *Religion and the Scientific Method.* Dordrecht, Holland: D. Reidel Publishing Company, 1977, pp. 173-82.

Swinburne, Richard. *The Concept of Miracle*. London: Macmillan, 1970, pp. 23-33.

Yandell, Keith. "Miracles, Epistemology and Hume's Barrier." *International Journal for Philosophy of Religion* 7 (1976): 391-96.

CHAPTER IV

Can We Know That an Event Has Been Caused by God?

IV

CAN WE KNOW THAT AN EVENT HAS BEEN CAUSED BY GOD?

We are still considering the question of whether a miracle—if defined as an inexplicable direct act of God—can be identified. This question, we have seen, actually breaks down into three more specfic questions:

(1) Did the event in question actually occur as reported?

(2) Is the event permanently inexplicable scientifically?

(3) Was the event directly caused by God?

In Chapter II, we concluded that (1) must be answered on a case by case basis. In Chapter III, we discussed (2), concluding that permanently inexplicable events are not identifiable and, thus, that theists desiring to maintain that the miraculous can be identified must either settle for 'present inexplicability' or drop the reference to scientific explicability altogether. The purpose of this chapter is to discuss (3).

I

Would it ever be justifiable to maintain that an event which we all agree has occurred is in fact a direct act of God? This question must be considered from two important perspectives:

(3a) Would it ever be most plausible for all rational individuals to affirm that God has directly intervened?

(3b) Would it ever be justifiable for theists to maintain that God has directly intervened?

(3b) is obviously much weaker than (3a) since the affirmation of (3b) is consistent with the claim that nontheists can justifiably deny that God has directly intervened in any given situation while the affirmation of (3a) is not.

II

We will first consider (3a) in some detail. Are conditions conceivable under which all rational individuals would be forced to admit that God has directly intervened in earthly affairs? Tan Tai Wei is one of a number of philosophers who think so. Let us assume, Tan asks us, not only that Jesus called upon God to raise Lazarus and Lazarus arose, but that such feats were common in response to requests from Jesus for divine intervention. And let us further assume that such events have continued to occur frequently when divine intervention has been requested. Under these conditions, he argues, it would be unreasonable to continue indefinitely to seek for "an ordinary natural regularity that relates such exceptional events with the intentions and commands of this sort of religious personage."[1] At some point, the acknowledgement of supernatural intervention would be more rational "because here some of our ordinary criteria (which are independent of religious considerations), governing the rational acceptability of purported coincidences as merely ordinary ones, would not be met."[2]

Grace Jantzen argues in a similar manner:

> If a situation arose in which there were compelling evidence for believing that Jesus rose from the dead, a revision of our supposed natural laws would hardly be the appropriate response . . . Where there is a single exception to a perfectly well established and well understood law, and one that is inexplicable unless one appeals to divine intervention (in which case it assumes enormous significance), what can be gained by making the nomological read, "All men are mortal except those who have an unknown quality, observed on only one occasion and hitherto accountable for only by divine intervention." . . . The sceptical response would be inadequate.[3]

Neither Jantzen or Tan, it must be emphasized, is simply arguing that supernatural causation should be considered a plausible alternative when it cannot be shown that "nature left to her own devices could manage." Their claim is stronger: that if some conceivable events were to occur, the objective evidence would be such that it would be most reasonable for all rational individuals to assume that God has directly intervened.

Such reasoning, not surprisingly, has come under various forms of attack. Antony Flew, for example, believes that "for an hypothetical entity to find productive employment in a scientific theory that entity has to be so described that it becomes possible to deduce testable consequences of its existence and operations." But God, he points out, is believed by theists to be an infinite being, and "the infinite attributes which are an essential part of the idea (of God) must disqualify this concept from such workaday occupation."[4]

This criticism is weak. It may be true that if God is infinite, we can never totally comprehend his nature or accurately identify all his modes of behavior or understand completely why he does what he does. But the assumption that God is infinite does not, itself, rule out the possiblity that he has revealed to his finite creatures certain observable event sequences or patterns in relation to which they can (could) identify some of his activites—e.g., patterns related to petitionary prayer. In other words, there is nothing conceptually inconsistent in assuming that an infinite being has given his finite creatures enough information about some of his general modes of behavior to insure that they can in *some contexts* and *to some degree* correctly determine when he has directly intervened in his created order. Of course, to assume that God has in fact so revealed himself raises numerous epistemological questions (some of which we will consider later). But such questions are not related to the concept of divine infinitude Flew has in mind.

Flew, however, offers another criticism:

> The theist is only too eager, when hard pressed by criticism, to suggest that the ways of his God must necessarily be beyond our unaided understanding and conjecture. There is a price to be paid for whatever

> immunity is to be obtained by these means. Precisely in so far as, and for the same reasons that, the magnificant attributes specified ensure that nothing which occurs constitutes a falsification of the contention that there is such a Being: to that extent and by the same token it must become impossible to deduce any testable consequences of his existence.[5]

The essence of Flew's argument seems to be that since 'God exists' is a nonfalsifiable statement for the theist—i.e., since the theist is unwilling to let any occurrence count as evidence against the statement 'God exists'—she cannot consistently consider the statement 'God has caused event E' to be a testable (falsifiable) hypothesis—i.e., she cannot consistently claim that empirical evidence can establish (or refute) the claim that God has caused some event.

In one sense, this contention is simply false. It could be, for example, that Jantzen's belief in God's existence is nonfalsifiable while her belief that God literally raised Jesus from the dead is falsifiable. That is, while she might not be able to stipulate any set of conditions under which she would deny God's existence, she might well be able to stipulate numerous possible sets of conditions—e.g., the discovery of new historical data of various sorts—under which she would deny as well as affirm that God had *literally* raised Jesus from the dead. There would certainly be nothing inconsistent in such a stance.

However, we are not presently discussing what the theist can consistently affirm about God or his actions. We are trying to decide whether the objective evidence related to some event could be such that all rational individuals (not just those who had previously been theists) would have to acknowledge that divine intervention was the most plausible causal hypothesis. But to argue that objective evidence can establish divine intervention is, of course, to argue that such evidence can establish God's existence, for one certainly cannot affirm that God has intervened if one does not also affirm that God exists.

Accordingly, Flew is perfectly justified in raising the falsifiability issue in this context. It certainly would be unjustifiable for the theist to claim that 'objective' evidence can establish that God has intervened but then refuse, in principle, to allow any 'objective' evidence to count against his or her belief in God's existence. Moreover, Flew is certainly correct to argue that 'God exists' is a nonfalsifiable statement for many theists. But Flew gives us no reason to believe that all, or most, of those theists who consider divine causation to be a testable hypothesis—e.g., Jantzen and Tan—do not also consider God's existence a testable hypothesis. And unless he establishes this fact, his 'falsifiability' criticism has no relevance in the present context.

Finally, Flew questions the objectivity of any attempt to identify direct acts of God. "Without benefit of particular revelation," he tells us, we cannot know what God "might reasonably be expected to do." But the authentication of any specific form of revelation such as the Bible, he argues, is necessarily a subjective, sectarian matter.[6]

Flew is certainly justified in emphasizing the importance of revelation in this context. Since God, as defined by classical Christian theology, is not empirically observable, it may well be that unless such a being were in some manner to reveal to us those observable event patterns or event sequences in relation to which his activity could be identified, we could have no justifiable epistemological basis upon which to argue that any given observable occurrence was in fact the result of divine intervention. In short, it seems plausible to argue that one cannot maintain that God has directly intervened without also maintaining that some form of 'divine revelation' is in fact authentic.

But Flew seems to be implying more. He seems also to be arguing that the authenticity of some such revelation would have to be affirmed *before* (prior to the time that) any justifiable attempt to identify a direct act of God could be made. If he is correct, then the line of reasoning proposed by philosophers such as Tan and Jantzen faces a serious problem. Tan and Jantzen are arguing, remember, that if some conceivable events were to occur, all rational individuals (whether they had previously been theists or nontheists) would have to acknowledge that God has directly intervened. But if one must acknowledge the authenticity of some revealed pattern of divine activity *before* one can justifiably maintain that some observable occurrence has in fact been divinely caused, then belief in God's existence (as the Revealer of the relevant divine action pattern) must occur *prior to* the time that any attempt to identify a direct act of God is made. And, of course, if this is true, Tan and Jantzen are wrong to argue that the rational nontheist would, if faced with certain conceivable occurrences, be forced to acknowledge divine intervention—i.e., be forced to give up her nontheism. Only those *believers* who had previously acknowledged the authenticity of the revealed divine action pattern in question would have a justifiable basis for identifying any such occurrence as a direct act of God.

It seems to us, however, that Tan and Jantzen may have a plausible response open to them. When they discuss the apologetical power of certain conceivable occurrences—e.g., the resurrection of Jesus—they may not simply be arguing that such occurrences would establish that God exists and has intervened. They may well be arguing that such occurrences would establish simultaneously that (a) God exists, (b) certain of his revealed divine action patterns are authentic, and (c) at least one of these patterns has been instantiated. In other words, Tan and Jantzen may well be arguing that there are conceivable situations in which both the authenticity of a 'revealed' divine action pattern and its instantiation would have to be affirmed simultaneously by all rational individuals.

If this is what they mean, then they can grant the innocuous claim that divine causation cannot be affirmed *apart from* the affirmation of some revelatory claim, and yet deny the damaging claim that one must commit oneself to the authenticity of some revealed divine action pattern—that is, that one must be a believer—*before* one can have a justifiable basis for acknowledging that God has directly intervened.

There is also a problem with Flew's claim that the affirmation of any particular form of revelation is necessarily a subjective, arbitrary matter. If we have captured their intent, Tan and Jantzen are not arguing that the evidence inherent in any conceivable occurrence would objectively establish the authenticity of any particular form of revelation taken as a whole. They are not arguing, for example, that if it could be shown that Jesus rose from the dead, the authenticity of the Bible as a divine revelation would be objectively established. Their claim is much weaker: that in some conceivable contexts, some specific revelatory claims concerning specific divine action patterns—claims which may appear in the official revelatory organs of numerous, even mutually exclusive, systems of religion—could be objectively established as authentic.

We must conclude then that Flew's 'revelatory criticism' is also inadequate. This in no sense means, however, that we agree with Tan and Jantzen. There may well be conceivable situations which, *when considered in isolation*, make divine intervention a plausible causal hypothesis. But, of course, no actual event and, thus, no causal hypothesis for it, can be considered in isolation from the rest of phenomenal reality. Let us assume, for example, that a remarkable healing occurs in the context of fervent petitions to God. To acknowledge divine intervention in this context would also be to acknowledge implicitly that God's existence is compatible with other relevant experiential data—e.g., to acknowledge that God's existence is compatible with the evil we experience, the evidence for naturalistic evolution, the evidence for determinism, etc.

Accordingly, if such a 'healing' were to occur, the crucial question would *not* be, as Tan and Jantzen imply, whether divine causation is the most plausible causal explanation for this event alone. The crucial question would be whether divine causation is the most plausible explanation, given all that this implies for that common set of human experiences of which this specific occurrence is simply one member.

Now let us assume that in comparing the plausibility of affirming that God has healed the individual in question (and, thus, that God's existence is compatible with the amount and types of evil in the world) with the plausibility of affirming that God's existence is not compatible with *all* that we commonly experience (and, thus, that God did not heal the individual in question) someone decides that God's nonexistence is more plausible overall. In other words, let us assume that the *prima facie* evidence for God's existence which has been generated by the 'healing' in question is not of sufficient weight in the mind of a given individual to make the theistic perspective the most plausible explanation for all common phenomenal reality. Could Tan or Jantzen justifiably accuse such an individual of being stubborn or intellectually dishonest or irrational? It is by no means obvious that they could. At the very least, they would have to furnish us with additional argumentation at this point.

This same problem can be stated in a slightly different way. To argue that God's activity is the most plausible causal hypothesis for a given event is really to argue that this event can establish the superiority of the theistic world view. In other words, to see direct divine intervention as the most plausible causal explanation in the test cases offered by Tan and Jantzen is to see theism as a more plausible world view than naturalism. But it is by no means obvious that an appeal to one event in isolation from all other common experience will be very effective in establishing the superiority of either of these world views. Unusual events of the type mentioned by Tan and Jantzen are seen by some philosophers as a justifiable component in a cumulative case for Christian theism.[7] But Tan and Jantzen need to give us reasons for believing that the consideration of any isolated instance alone could rationally establish the superiority of the world view they favor.

However, perhaps even this grants too much to Tan and Jantzen. Many philosophers of science and religion argue that there are no neutral, objective facts or empirical events by which we can adjudicate between rival theoretical schemes. All data, they claim, is theory-laden. If they are correct, then world views might simply be different ways of seeing the same world. It may, in other words, be more of a matter of our world view commitments determining what we experience (and even what constitutes an experience) rather than the other way around. And if this is the case, evidence cannot, in principle, count for or against any world view, and any attempt to rationally and objectively move from experience to the God hypothesis is, in principle, doomed to failure.

But what if we drop the claim that empirical evidence could demonstrate that God—defined as the omnipotent, perfectly good creator of all—has intervened and argue rather for a much weaker claim: that conditions are conceivable under which it would be most plausible for all rational individuals to assume that some nonembodied rational agent has caused a given state of affairs. To do so would certainly avoid many of the problems associated with 'Godly intervention'. Assume, for example, that all Americans, at 1:00 p.m. EST, hear a 'voice from the sky' stating that total darkness will occur from 1:05-1:10 p.m. and that such darkness does at the appropriate time occur. To attempt to argue that this state of affairs has been caused by God would, as we have seen, embroil us in problems related to the specific identity, moral nature and power of such a being. But if we attempt rather to argue only that this state of affairs has been caused by a nonembodied, rational agent, the situation is much different. It no longer becomes necessary to identify the entity in question—i.e., distinguish between this entity and other entities of this type—so the availability of an accurate 'divine action pattern' is not needed. And since it is no longer necessary to assume that the agent in question is all powerful or wholly good, issues related to divine infinitude and evil also become irrelevant. We need only establish that this state of affairs is most likely the result of the intentional activity of some being which cannot be detected empirically.

But could even this much ever be demonstrated to the satisfaction of most rational individuals? It depends on one's ontological commitments. If an individual is firmly committed, for example, to the belief that all reality is composed of 'matter' in various forms, it is very unlikely that any conceivable state of affairs would convince him or her that a nonembodied, rational agent—if defined as some sort of nonmaterial being—exists and has intervened in earthly affairs. For others, however, a positive response may be possible. Since belief in the existence of a nonembodied rational entity does not entail belief in any form of deity or creator, to affirm the existence of such an entity would be consistent with the basic ontological assumptions of many nontheistic and theistic perspectives.

But, of course, once we grant that such a nonembodied rational intervener need not be a 'god' of any sort, the possibility of intervention by such a being becomes irrelevant to the concept of miracle. For the concept of miracle, as normally understood, involves *divine* causation.

Accordingly, it seems best to conclude *in this context* that (3a) cannot be answered affirmatively. It may be that certain occurrences, *if considered in isolation*, would appear to be best explained by an appeal to intervention by God or some other type of deity. But the key question, we have seen, is not whether it is most plausible to believe in the existence and interventive activity of God or some other deity, given a single occurrence (or set of occurrences). The key question is whether it is most plausible to believe in the existence and interventive activity of God or some other deity, given *all* that we commonly experience. And one's answer to this question, we have argued, may not depenc as much on the ''evidence' as it does on one's 'perspective'.

But what of (3b)? Would it ever be justifiable for theists to maintain that God is directly responsible for some state of affairs? If we assume God's existence for the sake of our discussion, the question actually becomes:

(3b') Given that God exists, would it ever be justifiable for theists to maintain that he has directly intervened in earthly affairs?

Many theists believe the answer to be yes. They believe that they possess accurate information about God's general 'patterns of action' in our world. And, thus, they believe that if they were to see some specific event fit such a pattern, they could justifiably label it a direct act of God. Or, stated more formally, they believe that (3b') can be answered affirmatively because they affirm the following:

(4) A necessary and sufficient condition for the identification of an occurrence as a direct act of God is that the state of affairs in question fit (instantiate) an accepted divine action pattern—i.e., be consistent with accepted conditional statements which describe when (and sometimes how) God directly intervenes—and this condition can, at least in principle, be satisfied.

Before evaluating this contention, some clarifications are necessary. First, it may be helpful to illustrate how (4) would in fact function. Consider the following situation. John, a believer, has grown up in a home in which the Bible is accepted as literally true. He has been taught, accordingly, that if one prays to God in time of trouble, God will directly answer. In other words, John believes he has acquired 'knowledge' of a specific divine behavior pattern related to petitionary prayer. One day John finds himself in a serious personal crisis. His little girl is gravely ill, and there seems little hope for her recovery. John prays to God, beseeching that he save her life. Happily, the next day the girl is inexplicably improved and later goes on to make a full recovery. Given his affirmation of (4), John feels justified in labeling the unusual recovery a direct act of God as the state of affairs in question seems clearly to him to instantiate a previously accepted pattern of how God directly interacts with his creation.

But consider the following situation. Jim, a believer, also has what he believes to be a thorough knowledge of the various divine action patterns. One he day notices a peculiar phenomenon in his garden: his vegetables continually grow from seed to full maturity in one hour and then quickly regress again to seed. Try as he will—e.g., discuss the state of affairs with respected botanists—Jim can find no specific natural cause for the strange phenomenon. Moreover, Jim is also aware of no divine action pattern into which this unusual phenomenon can be placed. Thus, given his affirmation of (4), he must at present rule out one possibility: that the phenomenon can justifiably be labeled (identified as) a direct act of God.

Two further clarifications are also necessary at this point. First, few theists would wish to argue that God can only act in accordance with recognized divine action patterns—i.e., can only intervene when a recognized set of antecedent causal conditions has been met. For example, although divine healing in response to human petitions or an attitude of faith is a recognized divine action pattern, few theists would wish to contend that God cannot directly heal an individual unless he is petitioned to do so or unless the afflicted individual (or some other individual) displays enough faith. Most would want to insist rather that God can heal individuals whenever he desires for whatever reasons he deems acceptable and that he is under no compulsion to make clear to the believer why or how he does so. (4), it should be explicitly noted, is consistent with this fact as there is no claim therein that all direct acts of God must fit within recognized divine action patterns. The relevant claim in (4) is much weaker: that the instantiation of a recognized divine action pattern is a necessary condition for the *indentification* of a direct act of God.

Second, few theists would contend that God must always intervene in a predictable manner. That is, few theists hold that God must always bring about the expected or desired consequent, given the instantiation of the antecedent causal conditions in a recognized divine action pattern. For example, although divine healing in the response to human petition is for many theists a recognized divine action pattern, few theists would wish to maintian that God must necessarily heal an individual if he is petitioned to do so. (4) is also consistent with this fact as the relevant claim therein is only that, if both the antecedent conditions and the consequent of a recognized divine action pattern are in fact instantiated, such instantiation is a sufficient condition for *identification* of the consequent as a direct act of God.

(4), however, is problematic. First, the assumption by the proponent of (4) that he or she does in fact possess accurate knowledge of various divine action patterns is, of course, debatable. Theists not only differ greatly with respect to which 'holy writings' contain such information, they also differ greatly with respect to how such writings are to be interpreted. But, even if we grant a theist the accuracy of the divine action patterns she or he affirms, (4) is, in the last analysis, simply too strong.

This is most easily seen in relation to those occurrences which seemingly fit divine action patterns and yet are instances of event types which are presently explicable scientifically. Consider for example, a situation in which the only house in the path of a tornado which is not destroyed is the one in which a believer is fervently praying for deliverance. This state of affairs would clearly instantiate a recognized divine action pattern and, thus, given (4), the believer in question could justifiably consider her 'deliverance' a direct act of God. But in actuality, of course, such epistemological certainty would be unwarranted. For, given the well-documented fact that tornadoes frequently 'spare' homes in their paths when petitioning is not a factor, the believer in question could have no certainty that her home was spared because God directly intervened. That is, she could not justifiably claim in this case that the instantiation of a recognized divine action pattern was in fact a sufficient condition for the identification of the consequent as a direct act of God.

(4) is also problematic in relation to presently inexplicable occurrences. Assume, for example, that cancer cells immediately disappear from the body of a believer shortly after God is petitioned to heal him. This state of affairs would clearly instantiate a recognized divine action pattern and, thus, given (4), the believer in question could justifiably consider it a direct act of God. But, as we have seen, all individuals must acknowledge a necessarily limited understanding of the natural laws which operate in our universe, even if it is assumed that God is the author of such laws. Accordingly, although

the 'healing' in question might not be presently explicable, the believer in question could not claim with certainty that it was the result of direct divine intervention rather than the result of some presently unrecognized natural law—e.g., a psychosomatic law of some sort. In short, the claim that (4) is a sufficient condition for the identification of a direct act of God would again be too strong.

And, finally, (4) is problematic because, given the historical fact that believers have often been forced to admit that event types which were once strongly believed to be explicable primarily in terms of God's interventive activity—e.g., human conception—are in fact now explicable scientifically, the real possibility of natural causation must be taken serious by the believer in every case.

But what if we read (3b') more weakly? Instead of asking whether theists could, in principle, identify direct acts of God with something approaching epistemological certainly, what if we simply ask whether theists could, in principle, justifiably maintain that it is more likely than not that a given occurrence is a direct act of God? This does change things slightly. If we assume that God exists, and that a given theist has accurate information about his action patterns, then, given the seeming instantiation of such a pattern, such a theist may well be justified in maintaining, herself, that the event in question is probably a direct act of God. But given our necessarily limited human understanding of the 'natural' order, it would not be justifiable for such a theist to maintain that all other theists must also see the event in this light. It would always remain justifiable for other theists to maintain at the very least that no determination can be made.

Or, to state this important point somewhat differently, if a theist argues only that the instantiation of a divine action pattern is a sufficient condition for justifiably maintaining that the event in question is probably a direct act of God, it may be justifiable for her to believe a given occurrence to be the result of divine intervention. But, given the inherent evidential ambiguity caused by our limited human perspective, it remains within the epistemic rights of other theists to choose not to affirm such intervention in any given case.

There is, however, another criterion for the identification of direct acts of God to consider. Religious writings describe numerous cases in which 'men of God' possessed the ability or power to immediately identify direct acts of God. Accordingly, it might be argued that:

(5) The fact that a state of affairs is a direct act of God is self-authenticating (self-evident) to the spiritually perceptive person.

Some aspects of (5) are nonproblematic. Few persons would deny that some theists truly believe that they can clearly intuit (perceive) direct acts of God. And if we grant to the theist that God exists and personally communicates with believers, there seems little reason to deny, in principle, that this form of spiritual intuition (perception) could occur.

It is a matter of historical fact, however, that the 'self-authenticating' religious perceptions of one theist will frequently contradict the 'self-authenticating' religious perception of other, equally sincere theists. Therefore, we must assume that not all purportedly self-authenticating religious perceptions are veridical. But if misperception is possible, how is the theist to decide which of his seemingly self-authenticating religious experiences are veridical and which are not? Or how is the observer to decide which 'self-authenticating' claims to accept as veridical and which to reject? The only viable alternatives to admitting epistemological uncertainty, it would appear, are for the theist to either use some objective standard to test the perceptions in question—e.g., check such perceptions against recognized divine action patterns—or argue that he is able in some way to intuit directly which, if any, of the perceptions in question are in fact veridical—i.e., simply reaffirm some form of (5). But the former response is subject to the types of epistemological difficulties inherent in (4) while the latter response simply begs the question. In short, (5) is too subjective to be of much value in the present context.

What ought we conclude, then, with respect to (3b)? We must conclude, it seems, that while theists may under some circumstances be able justifiably to affirm, for themselves, that God has directly intervened, it cannot be argued that conditions exist under which all theists would be forced to admit that God has directly done so.

NOTES

[1]Tan Tai Wei, "Recent Discussions on Miracles," *Sophia* II (October, 1972): 24.

[2]Ibid.

[3]Grace Jantzen, "Hume on Miracles, History and Politics," *Christian Scholar's Review* 8 (1979): 325.

[4]Antony Flew, *God and Philosophy* (New York: Dell Publishing Company, 1966), p. 151.

[5]Ibid., p. 152.

[6]Ibid., pp. 151-158.

[7]See, for example, William Abraham, *An Introduction to Philosophy of Religion* (Englewood, N. J.: Prentice Hall, 1985), pp. 98-113; Basil Mitchell, *The Justification of Religious Belief* (London: Macmillan, 1973), pp. 39-57.

SELECTED BIBLIOGRAPHY

Chapter IV

Abrahams, William. *An Introduction to Philosophy of Religion*. Englewood, N.J.: Prentice Hall, 1985, pp. 98-113.

Ahern, Dennis. "Miracles and Physical Impossibility." *Canadian Journal of Philosophy* 7 (March, 1977): 71-79.

Basinger, David. "Miracles and Apologetics: A Response." *Christian Scholar's Review* 9 (1980): 348-53.

Basinger, David. "Christian Theism and the Concept of Miracle: Some Epistemological Perplexities." *The Southern Journal of Philosophy* 18 (1980): 137-50.

Brown, Colin. *Miracles and the Critical Mind*. Grand Rapids: Eerdmans, 1983, pp. 281-242.

Chryssides, George D. "Miracles and Agents." *Religious Studies* 11 (September, 1975): 319-27.

Fern, Richard L. "Hume's Critique of Miracles: An Irrelevant Triumph." *Religious Studies* 18 (September, 1982): 337-54.

Ferre, Fredrick. *Language, Logic and God*. New York: Harper and Brothers, 1961, pp. 44-50.

Fethe, Charles. "Miracles and Action Explanations." *Philosophy and Phenomenological Research* 36 (March, 1976): 415-22.

Geisler, Norman. *Miracles and Modern Thought*. Grand Rapids: Zondervan, 1982.

Jantzen, Grace. "Hume on Miracles, History and Politics." *Christian Scholar's Review* 8 (1979): 318-25.

Mitchell, Basil. *The Justification of Religious Belief*. London: Macmillan Press, Ltd., 1973, pp. 39-57.

Nowell-Smith, Patrick. "Miracles—The Philosophical Approach." *The Hibbert Journal* 48 (June, 1950): 354-60.

Swinburne, Richard. *The Concept of Miracle*. London: Macmillan, 1970, pp. 53-64.

Wei Tan Tai. "Recent Discussions on Miracles." *Sophia* 11 (October, 1972): 21-28.

Wisdom, John. "Gods." In *In Religious Language and the Problem of Religious Knowledge*, ed. Ronald Santoni. Bloomington, Ind.: Indiana University Press, 1968.

Young, Robert. "Miracles and Credibility." *Religious Studies* 16 (December, 1980): 465-68.

CHAPTER V

Should Theists Expect Miraculous Divine Intervention?

V

SHOULD THEISTS EXPECT MIRACULOUS DIVINE INTERVENTION?

Thus far we have basically been treating the miraculous as an isolated concept. But to talk of miracles this way is somewhat misleading for miracles do not exist in a vacuum. They function theoretically as a part of the broader theistic conceptual scheme and practically as events in the lives of individual believers. Therefore, any examination of the miraculous cannot be complete until we explore that extent to which miracles can be coherently related to other theistic concepts, beliefs and practices. Our purpose in this chapter is to raise and examine some issues and problems that emerge when this is done.

Most classical Christian theists make the distinction (first mentioned in Chapter I) between direct and indirect acts of God. God, they believe, has created the universe, established the 'laws' upon which causal interaction within the universe is based, and continues to sustain such interaction by his power. Most earthly occurrences are seen as flowing from this natural order. Such events, called *indirect* acts of God, are thought to be characterized by regularity and consistency and, thus, the world is seen as open to 'natural' explanations. Science is possible. Moreover, these indirect acts of God are believed to be in a sense impersonal to individual persons. To use biblical language, "it rains," it is believed, "on the just and the unjust." Or to use the language of providence, to speak of God's activity in this world is normally, it is held, to speak of God's general providence.

But most classical theists also maintain that there are some events which would not have occurred if God had not *directly* intervened, that is, if he had not at some point and in some manner circumvented or modified the general cause/effect patterns he has established. Miracles, as stated earlier, are usually thought to fall within this 'direct act of God' category. Thus, for such theists, to confront the miraculous is to confront the irregular, unpredictable and the scientifically inexplicable. Miracle becomes a means through which God can act in a direct and, hence, special way in the world. Through miracles God can correlate events in nature with the specific needs of particular persons. In the language of providence, to speak of miracles is for such theists to speak of God's special providence.

The possibility of the occurrence of miracle is of course no problem for anyone who accepts this traditional theistic view of the God/world relationship. If God has designed, created and maintains the natural world, he certainly has the power to miraculously intervene if and when he so desires. However, once we move beyond the bare possibility of miracle, another, more interesting question emerges: To what extent can such theists expect God's miraculous activity in nature?

While classical theists ground the possibility of miracle in God's power (omnipotence), the probability that God will work miracles is usually grounded in God's goodness (omnibenevolence and justice). The God of

Christian theism, it is argued, is not the impersonal, disinterested God of deism. Within the Christian tradition, God is conceived as a Parent who is interested in the world and as a result is personally and constructively involved in the world. Like an earthly parent, God guides, rewards, aids and disciplines his children. And this involvement goes beyond his general care: it is individual, special and direct. Thus, to the extent to which miracle is a way through which God can express his special concern for his children, miracle can and should be expected.

However, for theists to ground their expectation for miracles in God's goodness generates a serious problem. While it is easy to attribute goodness to God when he miraculously prevents a specific evil, what are we to make of God's goodness when no such action takes place? Doesn't this mean that God wants these evils to occur? For instance, if the recovery of a sick child is attributed to God's miraculous activity, must we not conclude that God wants every other child who dies to die? After all, these deaths could have been divinely prevented. If a miracle-working God can do as he pleases in nature, it appears we have no choice but to assign responsibility for specific evils to God. But if God is responsible for specific evils, how can he be good? In short, a miracle-working God "creates enormous problems for theodicy for it makes God responsible for every preventable natural evil."[1]

Some theists—feeling the force of this argument—reject classical theism and its notion of miracle. The process theist, for example, advocates a God who, in principle, cannot unilaterally bring about events in nature. For the process theist, miracle (as defined above) is a metaphysical impossibility. God, consequently, cannot be held responsible for the occurrence of specific evil events in nature. This move, however, can only be made by deviating from the classical notions of creation *ex nihilo*, divine self-existence and divine transcendence.[2]

Other theists attempt to solve the problem while remaining within the assumptions of classical theism. A popular way of doing this is to extend the traditional free will defense and develop what shall hereafter be called the 'uniformity defense'. Proponents of this uniformity defense argue that the classical Christian claim that God can directly and miraculously intervene in earthly affairs is ambiguous and, hence, misleading. While miracles are possible vis-a-vis divine power alone, their possibility must be qualified vis-a-vis other divine intentions for the world. More specifically, God's miraculous involvment in nature must be coherently related to God's intention to create free, rational and moral persons. And if nature is to support and make possible free, moral agents, it must be characterized, by and large, by order and uniformity. F. R. Tennant sums this up well:

> It cannot be too strongly insisted that a world which is to be a moral order must be a physical order characterized by law or regularity. The theist is only concerned to invoke the fact that the law-abidingness . . . is an essential condition of the world being a theatre of moral life. Without such regulari-

> ty in physical phenomena there could be no probability to guide us: no prediction, no prudence, no accumulation of ordered experience, no pursuit of premeditated ends, no formation of habit, no possibility of character or of culture. Our intellectual faculties could not have developed . . . And without rationality, morality is impossible.[3]

This of course implies that God's miraculous activity in nature must be minimized. Since to the extent to which God's activity in nature is regular and orderly it cannot be miraculous, the classical theist must minimize the occurrence of miracles in direct proportion to her emphasis on general providence. In other words, the very reason the classical theist has for emphasizing a regular and consistent natural order is *at the same time* a reason for minimizing the miraculous. While in the abstract the classical theist can (and must) affirm the possiblity of miracle, as C. S. Lewis (a staunch defender of the possibility of miracle) states, "the very conception of a common, and therefore, stable world demands that [miracles] be extremely rare."[4]

From this the proponent of the uniformity defense concludes that God is not directly responsible for not miraculously preventing all evils because this sort of providential activity cannot be coherently attributed to God. God cannot both will a uniform orderly nature and at the same time unilaterally control and, hence, plan how the realm of nature will relate to individual persons. If God were to use miracle to perfectly correlate nature to lives of individual free persons, he would undermine the very uniform natural order which He, in His wisdom and goodness, must will and maintain if a moral world is possible in the first place.

But if there is a limit to the amount of miraculous activity God can perform, the proponent of the uniformity defense continues, then God is not in total control of how nature affects particular persons. Hence, what occurs in nature in relation to free persons is not unilaterally determined by the divine will. And, consequently, when evils enter the lives of individuals, these evils need not be seen as special acts sent by God. They are possible and occur in the world only as unwanted but unavoidable by-products of a world order which, as a whole, is good.[5] And since these evils are not willed by God and, hence, not good in and of themselves, the classical theist is free to affirm the genuineness of this evil, the goodness of God and the human responsibility to work toward mitigating these evils.

Not all classical theists, however, look favorably on this 'uniformity defense'. After all, the uniformity defense works by minimizing God's special providence. Hence, the God of the uniformity defense is limited in his sovereign control over the details of human affairs. But in what sense can a limited God be omnipotent or perfect in power? Moreover, on a more practical level, if God's special providence must be minimized, what is left of God's personal and direct involvement in the lives of individuals? What happens to answers to prayer, healings and the many other special events in which Christians see the loving hand of God? Such a God appears to be either too weak or too far removed to meet the specific personal needs of individuals. In short, for many classical theists this 'solution' to the problem of evil comes at too high of a price.

Yet how is the classical theist to avoid the view of God implied in the uniformity defense? What aspect of the uniformity defense can be challenged? One strategy would be to call into question the belief that God's activity in nature must be characterized by regularity. In other words, the classical theist could call into question the belief that miracles must be minimized. On the whole, however, this is *not* the strategy used.

What is often challenged is the assumption within the uniformity defense that special providence must be equated with the miraculous. Must it be assumed that it is only through miraculous intervention that God can control how nature affects specific human affairs? If this can be successfully challenged, the door is open for simultaneously affirming *both* the uniformity of nature—i.e., the minimization of miracle—*and* God's special, providential control over how nature affects individuals. Divine omnipotence, interpreted as total control, can be preserved.

But how is it possible for God to work in a special yet nonmiraculous way? In what sense can an event flow predictably from the uniform order of nature and still be an event specially willed or sent by God? How can events in nature be specially correlated with the lives of individuals if God does not miraculously intervene in nature?

There are at least two ways classical theists try to answer these questions. On the one hand, some opt for theological determinism and an accompanying compatibilistic understanding of human freedom.[6] Within this viewpoint God totally determines the choices and actions of humans. Thus, it is possible for God to unilaterally correlate human choice and action with the uniform events in nature. God simply constructs the world in a such a way that events which are natural and uniform coincide with the lives of individual persons in the precise way he pleases. Thus, events in nature can be nonmiraculous—flow from the uniform and predictable order of nature—yet still be acts of special providence. Miracles can be minimized without minimizing special providence.

On the other hand, classical theists who have problems with such a thorough-going determinism argue that God foreknows (or timelessly knows) what free persons will freely choose. Thus, it was possible for God to design nature from the beginning in such a way that the events in nature will uniformly and predictably unfold in correlation with the actions and choices of free persons. Again, such events would be natural—i.e., nonmiraculous—yet still specially ordained and controlled by God. Applying this option to the problem of petitionary prayer, one classical theist explains:

> God has anticipated our prayers before the foundation of the world. He has built the answers to our prayers into the very structure of the universe . . . God put the universe together on the principle of personal relationships in which he answers prayer, and we can, in a measure, understand His loving provision only on the basis of His omniscience.[7]

Whether one opts for theological determinism or divine foreknowledge in this context, the result is the same. It becomes possible to label events as specially sent by God into the life of an individual *without* claiming that God miraculously intervened in nature to bring these events about. Thus, God's miraculous activity can be minimized without limiting God's special, providential control over how nature is correlated with particular human lives.

While we shall not explore the success of these two attempts, there are, however, several implications in their shared conclusion.[8] First, the distinction between general and special providence breaks down. While the metaphysical distinction between God's direct and indirect causal activity remains unchanged, whichever mode of action God chooses, the result will be *equally* providential. Miracles lose their providential uniqueness; natural events lose their impersonal ('natural') character. Events in nature, whether direct acts of God or indirect acts of God, regular or irregular, predictable or unpredictable, natural or supernatural, are *equally* under God's special providential control. Thus C. S. Lewis, while insisting that miracles are extremely rare, can go on to say, "all events are equally providential."[9]

Second, it follows that this view cannot be very easily reconciled with the way many Christian theists actually talk about God's providence. It is not uncommon for Christians to isolate certain events in their lives as 'special acts of God'. Of course to label an event as a special act of God only has meaning if we assume a backdrop of 'normal' or 'natural' events which occur in some sense apart from God's special, providential activity. In other words, Christians ordinarily assume that the distinction between special and general providence is meaningful and real. However, this assumption is not compatible with the view we are now analyzing. If we adopt this viewpoint, we have no recourse but to consistently talk about and act on the presumption that *all* that occurs has been specially willed by God.

Third, at this point the problem of evil once again raises its ugly head. If all that occurs in nature in relation to individuals flows directly and specially from the divine will, God is unavoidably responsible for the evil. God's sovereign control is preserved, but the genuineness of evil and the goodness of God are placed in jeopardy.

In conclusion, where does all this leave the classical theist? What has emerged are two basic approaches classical theists can take toward miracle, providence and evil. Both of these approaches accept the possibility of miracle. Moreover, both acknowledge that miracle must be minimized. In brief, both maintain there are good reasons why theists should *not* expect many miraculous interventions. The point of contention between these two views centers on one key question: Must special providence be equated with the miraculous?

For those who answer this question "yes," the door is open for developing the uniformity defense for evil and thereby arguing that God does not will the specific evils that occur in our lives. While this approach preserves God's goodness, it implies a notion of a God who is limited in the extent to which he can correlate the events in nature with the lives of particular persons. This certainly challenges the view many Christians have traditionally held concerning God's sovereignty and the extent of God's special involvement in the lives of individuals.

Those who answer "no" to this question—those who argue that special providence is not to be equated with miracle—are free to simultaneously affirm both the uniformity of nature and God's special providential control over the details of human lives. But this move has its price. It implies a God who is directly responsible for all specific evils. Moreover, this view challenges the distinction between general and special providence which is assumed in the way many theists talk about God's activity in their lives.

It would appear then that our discussion of miracle has left classical theists with a dilemma. They can affirm the pervasiveness of God's special providence in nature and try to explain in what sense evil is genuine and their God is good. Or they can argue that God cannot will specific evils and try to explain in what sense their God is to be considered omnipotent. But they cannot have it both ways—as some attempt or are perhaps tempted to try to do.

NOTES

[1]Frank Dilley, "Does the 'God Who Acts' Really Act?" *Anglican Theological Review* 47 (January 1965): 76; see also Brian Hebblethwaite, *Evil, Suffering and Religion* (New York: Hawthorne Books, 1976) p. 88, and J. C. Gaskin, "Miracles and Religiously Significant Coincidence," *Ratio* 17 (June 1975): 77-79.

[2]See David Basinger and Randall Basinger, "Divine Providence: Plantinga vs. Griffin," *Process Studies* 11 (Spring 1981): 11-24.

[3]*Philosophical Theology*.2 vols. (Cambridge: The University Press), 1928, 1929, 2: 199-200. For other formulations of the "uniformity defense", see Hebblethwaite, *Evil, Suffering and Religion*, Howard Burkle, *God, Suffering and Belief* (Nashville: Abingdon Press, 1977), Michael Peterson, *Evil and the Christian God* (Grand Rapids: Baker Book House, 1982) and Bruce Reichenbach, "Natural Evils and Natural Laws: A Theodicy for Natural Evils," *International Philosophical Journal* 16 (June 1976): 179-198.

[4]*The Problem of Pain* (New York: The Macmillan Co., 1962), p. 34.

[5]Tennant, 2: 204.

[6]See Robert Young, "Petitioning God," *American Philosophical Quarterly*, pp. 198-99.

[7]James Buwell, *A Systematic Theology of the Christian Religion* (Grand Rapids: Zondervan Publishing House, 1962), p. 61. See also Richard Westfall, *Science*

and Religion in Seventeenth Century England (Yale University Press, 1958), pp. 78-80, C. S. Lewis, *Miracles* (New York: Macmillan, 1947). pp. 180-187, Gaskin, pp. 77 and Young, p. 201.

[8]For an argument against speaking of "specially providential but non-miraculous events," see H. P. Owen, "Providence and Science," in *Providence*, edited by Maurice Wiles (London: SPCK, 1969), pp. 84-86.

[9]*Miracles*, p. 181. Cf. Aquinas, *Summa Contra Gentiles*, 111, 99 and Augustine, *The City of God*, x, 12, xxi, 9.

SELECTED BIBLIOGRAPHY

Chapter V

Basinger, David and Basinger, Randall. "Divine Providence: Plantinga vs. Griffin." *Process Studies* 11 (Spring, 1981): 11-24.

Basinger, David. "Human Freedom and Divine Providence: Some New Thoughts on an Old Problem." *Religious Studies* 15 (December, 1979): 491-510.

Brown, Colin. *Miracles and the Critical Mind.* Grand Rapids: Eerdmans, 1983, pp. 275-92.

Buswell, James. *A Systematic Theology of the Christian Religion.* Grand Rapids: Zondervan Publishing House, 1962.

Dilley, Frank. "Does the 'God Who Acts' Really Act?" *Anglican Theological Review* 47 (January, 1965): 66-80.

Gaskin, J.C. "Miracles and Religiously Significant Coincidence." *Ratio* 17 (June, 1975): 77-79.

Geisler, Norman. *Miracles and Modern Thought.* Grand Rapids: Zondervan, 1982.

Hebblethwaithe, Brian. *Evil, Suffering and Religion.* New York: Hawthorne Books, 1976.

Jantzen, Grace. "Miracles Reconsidered." *Christian Scholar's Review* 9 (1980): 354-58.

Lewis, C. S. *The Problem of Pain*. New York: Macmillan, 1962.

Peterson, Michael. *Evil and the Christian God*. Grand Rapids: Baker Book House, 1982.

Tennant, F. R. *Philosophical Theology*, 2 vols. Cambridge: The University Press, 1928, 1929.

Westfall, Richard. *Science and Religion in the Seventeenth Century England*. New Haven: Yale University Press, 1958.

Young, Robert. "Petitioning God." *American Philosophical Quarterly* 11 (July, 1974): 193-201.

INDEX

Problems in Contemporary Philosophy

1. Petra von Morstein, **On Understanding Works of Art: An Essay in Philosophical Aesthetics**
2. David and Randall Basinger, **Philosophy and Miracle: The Contemporary Debate**